THE LITTLE BOOK
OF
Knowledge

KING*fisher*

NEW YORK

KINGFISHER
Larousse Kingfisher Chambers Inc.
95 Madison Avenue
New York, New York 10016

First published in 2000
The material in this edition was previously published
in twelve individual volumes in 1992, 1993, and 1994

2 4 6 8 10 9 7 5 3 1

LIBRARY OF CONGRESS CATALOGING-IN-PUBLICATION DATA
has been applied for.

ISBN 0-7534-5299-5
Printed in China

CONTENTS

About This Book

Have you ever wondered where the stars came from, or how a plane flies? Maybe you would like to know who the Vikings were, or how a baby grows. If so, this book is for you!

The Little Book of Knowledge is filled with information about our world and the people who live in it. You can discover amazing facts about the natural world and the plants and animals you see around you. You can learn how people in other countries live and find out how you use science every day. You can even read about the unsolved mysteries of the Universe, such as how the Earth was formed and why the dinosaurs died out.

Every page holds something new for you to discover. Keep reading to find out about your fascinating world!

The
Universe

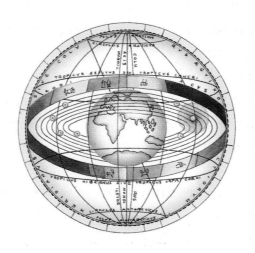

What is the universe?

The universe is everything that exists. The Earth is part of the universe. So are all the other planets and the Moon and Sun.

Stars and clouds of gas and dust called
nebulae are also part of the universe.
Scientists using telescopes and space probes
have learned a great deal about the universe
But there is still much that we do not know.

Spinning in space

Although we can't feel it, the Earth is always moving. It travels, or orbits, around the Sun. At the same time, the Moon is circling around the Earth. All the time, the Earth, Moon, and Sun are also spinning around themselves.

The Earth takes one year to orbit the Sun.

The Moon travels once around the Earth every 29 days and 13 hours.

The Sun, Moon, and Earth spin around on an imaginary line called an axis.

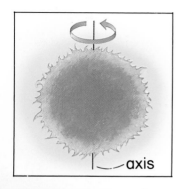

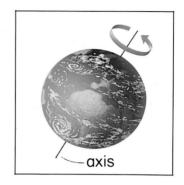

The Sun takes about a month to spin around once. The Earth takes 24 hours.

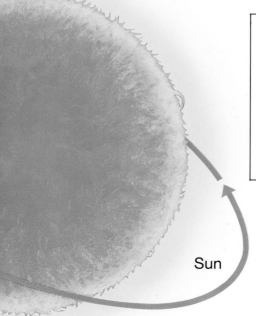

Sun

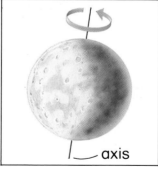

The Moon spins around once every 29 days and 13 hours.

The Sun, our star

prominence

As the Sun rises, the night stars fade in its bright light.

The Sun is a star, the closest star to us in the universe. Like all stars, it is a ball of hot, glowing gases.

Sometimes, jets of gas called prominences erupt from the Sun's surface. At other times, darker patches called sunspots appear. They look darker because they are much cooler than the rest of the Sun's surface.

sunspot

Remember: you must never look directly at the Sun, as it can damage your eyes.

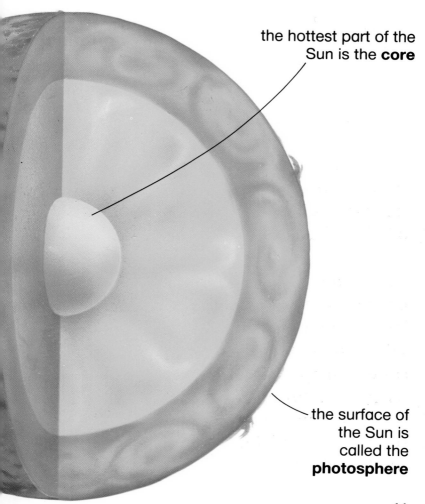

the hottest part of the Sun is the **core**

the surface of the Sun is called the **photosphere**

Day and night

The Earth is always spinning in space. As it spins around, first one side of its surface is turned toward the Sun, then the other. This is why we have day and night.

When our side of the Earth is turned to the Sun's light, it is our day.

People on the dark side of the Earth are having night.

north

south

summer

winter

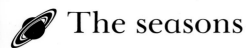 The seasons

It takes a year for the Earth to travel once around the Sun. As it moves around, the seasons change. This is because the Earth's axis is tilted at an angle.

When the northern half of the Earth is tilted toward the Sun, it is summer there. But in the south it is winter. Six months later, the southern half of the Earth is tilted toward the Sun. So in the south it is summer, but in the north it is winter.

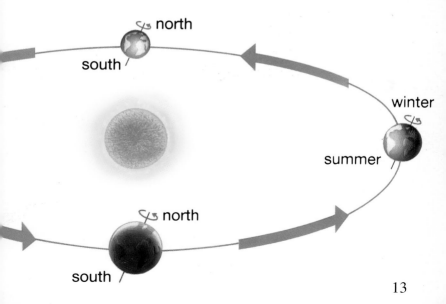

north

south

winter

summer

north

south

13

Our nearest neighbor

Moon

Earth

The Moon is our nearest neighbor
in space, but it is still about 240,000
miles away. Its surface is covered with lots
of craters and the sky above it is always
pitch black.

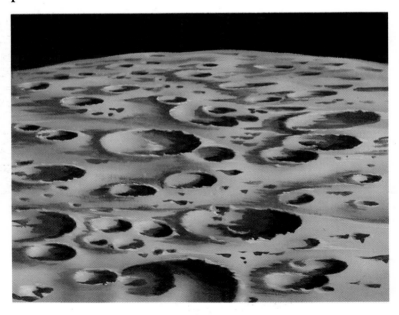

There is no air and no water on the Moon.
Without them, nothing can live there. The
craters were made when lumps of rock and
iron, called meteoroids, crashed into the
Moon's surface.

The changing Moon

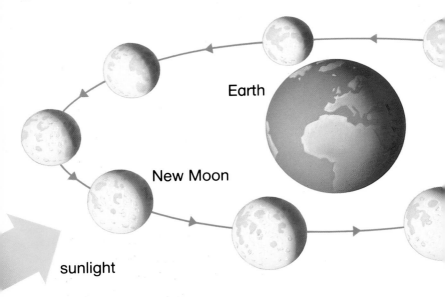

Earth

New Moon

sunlight

The Moon doesn't shine with its own light. We see it glowing in the sky because the light of the Sun shines on its surface. As the Moon travels around the Earth, all or part of it is lit up by the Sun. That is why, to us, the Moon seems to change shape.

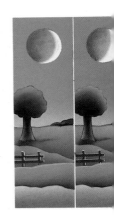

When the Moon lies between the Earth and the Sun, the side facing us is in darkness. We cannot see it at all. This is called a "New Moon." When the Moon is on the far side of the Earth from the Sun, we see all of one side lit up. We call this a "Full Moon."

Full Moon

From Earth, the Moon may seem to change shape, but in fact, it is always round. The changes in its shape are called the phases of the Moon.

The life of a star

A star is born when a cloud of gas and dust (1) shrinks into a ball (2). The ball gets hotter and hotter until it starts to glow as a newborn star. An average star shines for billions of years, burning up its gases (3). When it runs out of fuel, it swells up into a red giant (4). The red giant then starts to shrink (5 + 6) and becomes a white dwarf (7). The white dwarf slowly cools and fades to a cold black dwarf (8). Big stars turn into red supergiants (9). Instead of cooling down, they explode as supernovae (10) and for a short time burn more brightly than a billion Suns. What is left is either a neutron star (11) or, if the star was very big, a black hole (12).

3

2

1

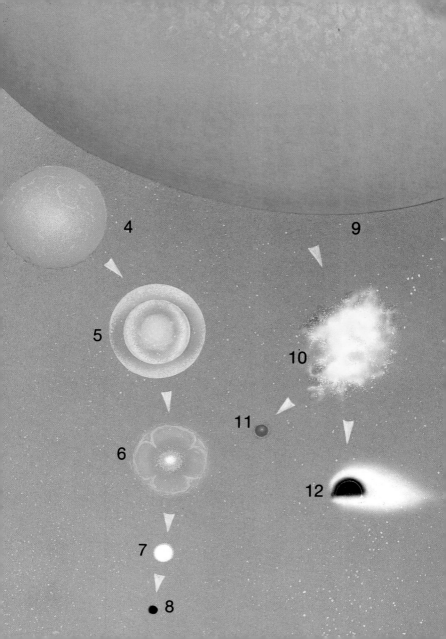

4

9

5

10

6

11

12

7

8

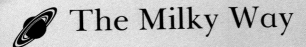 The Milky Way

If you look up at the sky on a clear night, you will see a ribbon of white crossing it. In this ribbon, stars lie so close together they form a single band of light. You are looking at a small part of the Milky Way. The Milky Way is the name of our galaxy—the huge group of stars that is our home in space.

This is what the Milky Way would look like from far out in space. It is a great spiral of stars in the shape of a pinwheel. Our Sun lies two thirds of the way out from the center of the galaxy. (In this picture the Sun is drawn bigger than it really is.)

Sun

The Sun's family

The Sun's family is called the solar system. It includes all the planets, moons, comets, and lumps of rock, dust, and ice that orbit the Sun. There are nine planets in the solar system.

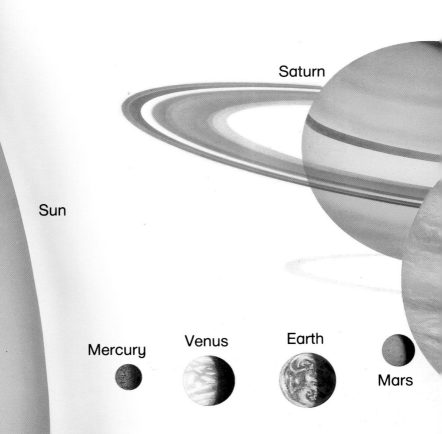

Saturn

Sun

Mercury

Venus

Earth

Mars

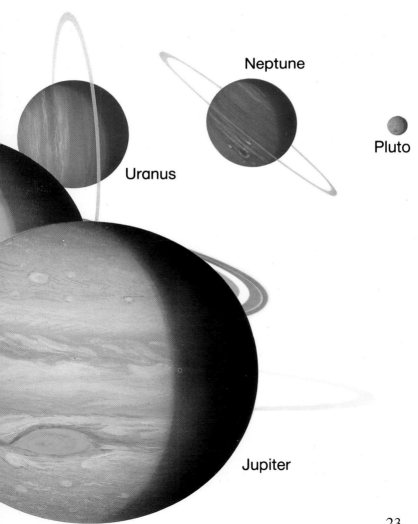

Neptune

Pluto

Uranus

Jupiter

Meteors

Sometimes a brief trail of fire shoots across the night sky. This is a meteor. A meteor is caused by a grain of dust from space. As it enters the blanket of gases that surrounds the Earth, the dust starts to burn up, leaving a glowing trail behind it.

There are also much bigger lumps of rock or iron called asteroids out in space. Millions of asteroids orbit the Sun between Mars and Jupiter.

asteroids

The biggest asteroids are hundreds of miles wide, others are quite small. Sometimes a lump of rock that was once part of an asteroid collides with the Earth. This is called a meteorite.

In 1908, a meteorite 100 feet wide exploded above Siberia, knocking down trees 30 miles away. About 40,000 years ago, a huge meteorite blasted out this great crater in Arizona.

Billions of galaxies

Our galaxy, the Milky Way, is just one of billions of other galaxies in the universe. Galaxies come in many shapes and sizes.

Spiral galaxies have arms that slowly revolve around a central ball of stars.

In a barred spiral
galaxy the arms
revolve around a
central bar of stars.

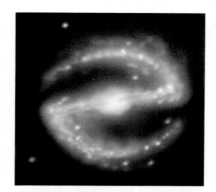

Some galaxies are
simply great balls of
stars. These are
called elliptical
galaxies. Usually,
they are made up of
very old stars.

Certain galaxies
don't seem to have
any shape at all.
They are called
irregular galaxies.

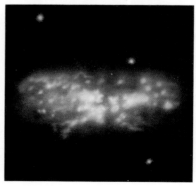

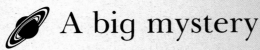 A big mystery

Scientists are fairly sure that the universe began with a huge explosion called the "Big Bang." They also believe that the universe is getting bigger as the galaxies move farther and farther apart. Perhaps the universe will just keep on growing for ever. Or perhaps one day the galaxies will start moving back together again and the universe will end in a "Big Crunch." Nobody knows.

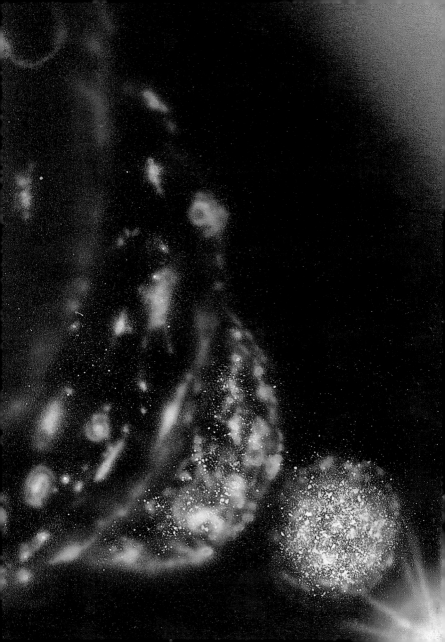

Amazing facts

Astronomers (scientists who study the stars, moon, planets, and other objects in Space) think there might be as many as 100 billion galaxies in the Universe.

The Sun is about 93 million miles from the Earth. It would take a jumbo jet 17 years to fly there.

Stars have different colors. White and blue stars are hottest. Yellow stars are cooler. Red stars are coolest of all.

Each of Saturn's rings is made up of dust and tiny pieces of ice and rock.

Our Planet Earth

🌍 What is Earth?

Our planet Earth is a huge,
rocky ball. It is one of
the nine planets that
travel around
the Sun.

If you were in
space, and you
could see
Earth, it would
look like this.

Earth looks blue
because most of it
is covered in water.
In fact, oceans, seas, and
lakes cover about seven
tenths of our planet's surface.

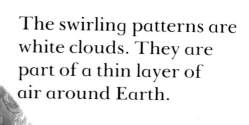

The swirling patterns are white clouds. They are part of a thin layer of air around Earth.

This layer of air is called the atmosphere.

As far as we know, Earth is the only planet that has air we can breathe.

🌍 Journey to the center

Earth is divided into three main parts:
the crust, the mantle, and the core.

1. The hard, rocky crust is about
25 miles thick under the land,
but only about 4 miles thick
under the sea.

2. The mantle is about 1,800
miles thick. It is hot, and
in some parts the rock
is melted. Melted or liquid
rock is called molten rock.

3. The core is even
hotter. It is about
2,600 miles thick.
The outer core is
made of liquid metal.
The inner core is the
hottest part. It is
made of solid metal.

🌐 Earthquakes

Earth's hard outer shell is divided into huge pieces called plates. The plates move very slowly. They are moved by currents in the molten rock underneath.

When the edges of two plates move suddenly, the ground shakes. We call this an earthquake. Earthquakes can make the land tremble so much that buildings fall down.

🌍 Volcanoes

A volcano is an opening in Earth's crust where molten rock can flow out. Molten rock is called magma when it is under the ground, and lava when it is on the surface.

When lava cools, it gets hard, and new rock is formed. Every time a volcano erupts, its lava makes another layer of rock. This is how some mountains are formed.

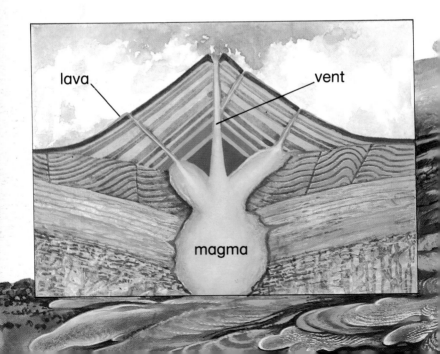

lava

vent

magma

🌍 Mountains

It takes millions of years for big mountain ranges to be formed.

Many mountains are formed when two plates push against each other. The rocks on the edges of the plates are squeezed together and pushed up into big folds.

Some mountains are still rising. They have jagged peaks. Older mountains have rounded peaks because they have been worn down.

🌍 What is air?

We cannot see it, taste it, or smell it, but air is all around us. Air is a mixture of invisible gases, mainly nitrogen and oxygen. People, animals, and plants need these gases to live. So if there was no air, there would be no life on Earth.

The air around Earth is called the atmosphere. It covers the whole planet like a blanket. It traps the heat from the sun to keep Earth warm. But it also protects us from the sun's harmful rays. Air is what brings different weather – hot and cold, wet and dry, windy and calm.

Higher up in the atmosphere, the air has less oxygen and nitrogen, and it gets colder. The air gradually gets thinner and thinner, until it ends and space begins.

🌍 The wind

When air moves we call it wind.

Heat from the sun warms the air and makes it rise.

Cold air moves in under the warm air, and a wind starts to blow.

Birds use warm air to glide through the sky. They hardly flap their wings, because the warm air carries them up.

Wind speeds are measured on the Beaufort scale.

Number 1 on the Beaufort scale is almost calm air. Number 4 is a breeze (about 15 miles per hour).

Number 7 is a moderate gale (about 35 miles per hour). Number 10 is a strong gale (about 60 miles per hour).

🌐 Storms

Thunderstorms bring wind and rain.
Fiercer storms, called hurricanes,
sometimes form over the oceans.
When they reach land, hurricanes.cause
enormous damage.

Tornadoes are whirlwinds that form over
land. As they spin along, they rip up trees
and buildings.

🌍 Lightning and thunder

Electricity builds up inside big, dark storm clouds. The lightning we see is a giant spark of this electricity.

Lightning often travels from a cloud right down to the ground. Lightning is dangerous because of its huge electrical power.

Seconds later, we hear thunder crashing.
Thunder is caused by lightning. When
lightning heats up the air, waves of air push
outward. This movement makes the
rumbling sound we hear.

We hear thunder after we see the lightning
because sound travels more slowly than
light through the air.

Rain

Raindrops form when the tiny droplets of water in clouds join together. When the drops become big and heavy, they fall to the ground.

Plants need water to grow. So rain is very important for growing crops for food. Without enough rain, crops may die and there may not be enough food for people and animals.

Rice is a plant that needs lots of water. Farmers grow rice in fields called paddies that have low walls to hold in the rainwater.

In very cold air, water droplets freeze around ice crystals and fall as hailstones.

🌐 Snow and ice

In cold places, water freezes into ice,
and snow covers the land and the trees.
A snowflake is made of many tiny ice
crystals that have become stuck together.

If you look at
snowflakes with a
magnifying glass,
you can see the
patterns of the
ice crystals.

🌐 Cold lands

The usual weather in a place is called its climate. Climate affects the land. Antarctica, around the South Pole, has a very cold climate, so it is covered in ice.

The Arctic, around the North Pole, is also covered in ice and snow. But in summer some of the snow melts, in regions called tundra. Plants grow, and herds of caribou come to graze. Insects hatch out, and birds fly in to nest.

🌐 Forests and woods

Huge forests of evergreen trees (which don't lose their leaves in winter) grow in the northern parts of the world, where winters are long and cold.

Other forests grow in countries with milder climates. Many trees in these forests are deciduous – they lose their leaves in winter.

The forests provide homes and food for many animals.

🌍 Grasslands

In places with long dry seasons it is mainly grass that grows. There are very few trees.

Australia's grassland is called the bush. Kangaroos feed on the grass there.

Many animals live on the African grasslands, which are called savannas.

🌏 Hot and dry

Deserts cover large parts of the world. They get very little rain, so they have few plants and animals — just a lot of sand and rock. Wind blows the sand into huge hills called dunes.

In some deserts, plant seeds lie in the ground for years. The seeds come to life only when there is a rainstorm.

Cactus plants in American deserts have thick, swollen stems that store water. They can live for months without any rain.

The jerboa is an animal that lives in the desert. It digs burrows underground and comes out to feed at night, when it is cool.

 Rain forests

Rain forests grow in countries that are hot and have a lot of rain. More than half of the world's plant and animal species, or kinds, live in these forests.

The rain forests are in danger because people are cutting them down and turning them into farmland.

🌐 Looking after Earth

Everyone can help to make Earth a clean and healthy place for all living things.

We can help to keep Earth beautiful by planting trees.

Trees provide food and homes for many animals. They also help to keep the air clean.

We can help to keep Earth clean by being careful about our garbage.

A lot of our garbage can be recycled.
Recycling means making new things from
old materials.

bottle banks

These pieces of
garbage can be
recycled.

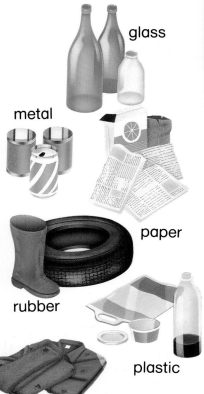

glass

metal

paper

rubber

plastic

old clothes

If we recycle our
empty glass bottles,
they can be melted
down to make new
glass.

Using things again
is less wasteful.
So recycling helps
to save Earth's
resources.

Amazing facts

🌍 The Earth is over four billion years old.

🌍 The world's highest mountain is Mount Everest, in the Himalayas. It stands on the border between two countries, Nepal and China, in Asia. It is 29,028 feet high.

🌍 The world's driest place is the Atacama desert in Chile, in South America. One part has not had any rain in 400 years.

🌍 Recycling one ton of paper can save 15 trees from being cut down to make new paper.

The Sea

Our blue planet

If you looked down at the Earth from space, you would see that most of our planet is covered by the ocean.

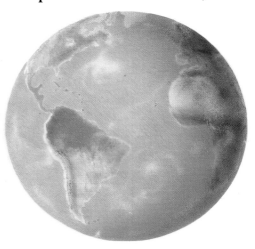

More than 70 percent of the Earth is covered in water.

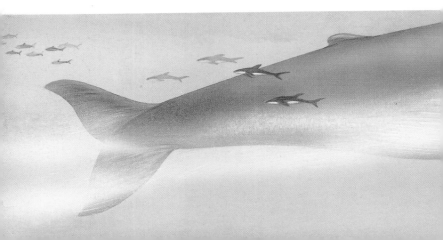

Life began in the ocean about 3,500 million years ago. Tiny plants produced a gas called oxygen. Oxygen made it possible for other forms of life to develop.

plankton

Now the ocean is home to millions of plants and animals—from tiny plankton to huge blue whales.

Oceans and seas

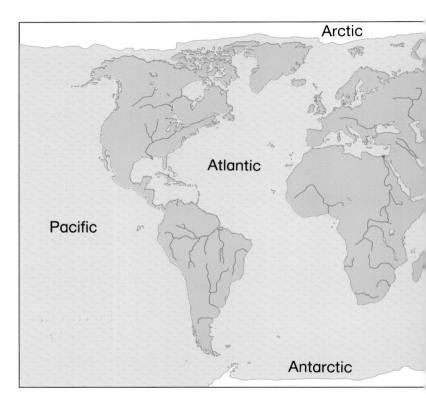

Arctic

Atlantic

Pacific

Antarctic

There is really only one ocean on the
Earth. This huge ocean is separated into
five smaller oceans by the continents.
The five oceans are the Pacific, Atlantic,
Indian, Arctic, and Antarctic Oceans.

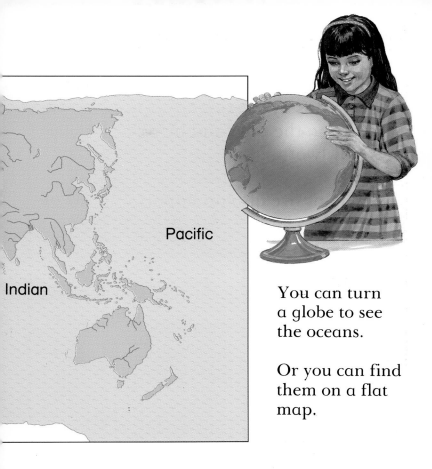

Pacific

Indian

You can turn
a globe to see
the oceans.

Or you can find
them on a flat
map.

Seas are parts of the oceans. The
Mediterranean, the Bering Sea, and the
Caribbean are the largest seas, but there
are also many others. (Sometimes people
say "sea" when they mean "ocean.")

71

Oceans and weather

The oceans help to control the climate. They do this by soaking up heat from the Sun during the day, and by releasing it very slowly at night.

The oceans are also an important part of the water cycle.

In the cycle, the Sun's heat turns some seawater into an invisible gas called water vapor. The vapor rises into the air. When it reaches cold air, the vapor turns into tiny drops of water.

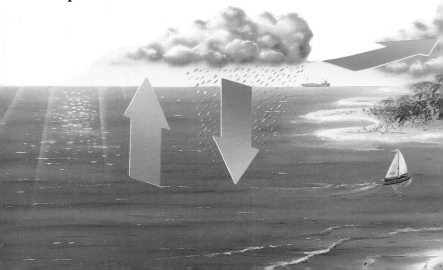

The drops of water join together and make clouds. The water in the clouds falls as rain, snow, or hail. Most of it falls into the oceans. But even when it falls on land, the water eventually flows back into the oceans.

Ocean currents

Currents are like huge rivers in the ocean. They carry water from one part of the world to another. Some currents flow near the surface. Icebergs drift on surface currents around the poles. Other currents flow deep down, along the seafloor.

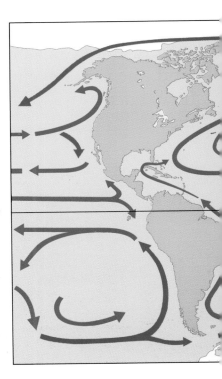

There are many surface currents. Some are warm and some are cold. They link up and make six large loops called gyres.

Strong winds in the tropics around the equator push the surface currents from east to west. Near the poles, winds push the currents back round again.

As the winds push them along, the currents bend around the continents and change direction.

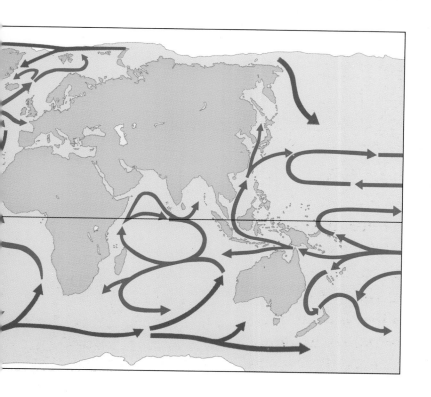

The tides

Moon

Earth

low
tide

high tide

Twice a day, tides make the oceans' water level rise and fall. During a high tide, the water moves farther onto the land. During a low tide, the water moves back.

What causes tides? The Moon's pull, and the Earth's spin.

On the side of the globe facing the Moon, the Moon's gravity pulls the oceans.

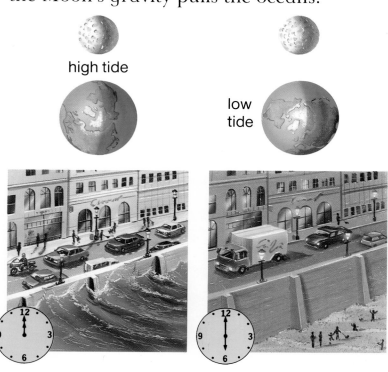

high tide

low tide

On the other side of the globe, the Moon's gravity pulls the Earth away from the oceans. So both places have high tides.

Every 24 hours the Earth spins right around. So most coasts have two high tides a day. Follow the red dot to see why.

🐚 The water's edge

Animals and plants that live on a rocky shore lead a double life. When the tide is in, they must live underwater. When the tide is out, they must survive in the air.

Barnacles and mussels live on the rocks. When the tide is in, these animals open their shells and stick out their feathery legs to catch plankton. Plankton are too small to see, but the water is full of them.

Snails and limpets come out of their shells and graze on the seaweed growing on the rocks. Starfish feed on the snails and the mussels. Crabs hunt for food too—they eat almost anything! Shrimp, anemones, and small fish live in pools that do not dry up.

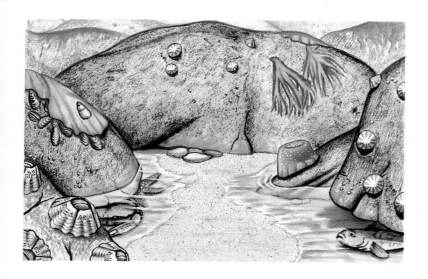

When the tide goes out, the snails and limpets cling to the rocks. Barnacles and mussels close their shells up tight. Crabs and starfish look for hiding places and wait for the next high tide.

Ocean zones

There are four main depth zones in the ocean. Different types of animals live in each zone.

The shallowest zone is called the epipelagic zone. Sunlight warms the water in this zone, and many plants live here. So many animals live here too, because they feed on the plants.

The next zone is called the mesopelagic zone. Sunlight barely reaches this far down, so plants cannot grow here. The animals living here must swim up to the epipelagic zone at night to feed.

In the bathypelagic and the really deep abyssopelagic zones, it is pitch dark. Very few animals live here. They must work hard to find food. Some eat particles of food that drift down from above. Some are skillful hunters.

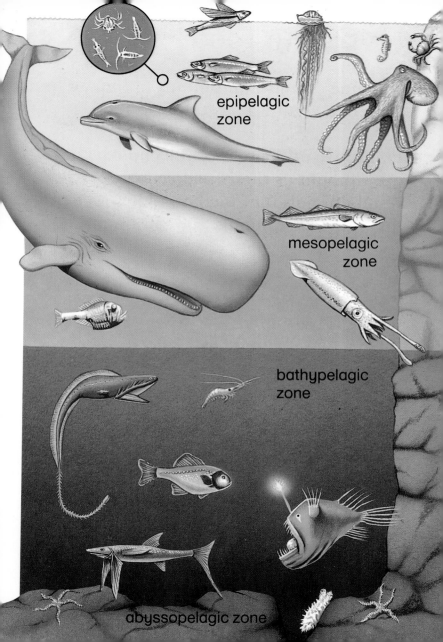

epipelagic zone

mesopelagic zone

bathypelagic zone

abyssopelagic zone

🐚 Ocean food

Imagine animals and plants in the sea as links in a chain. They all need food.

Plants are at the end of the chain. They use sunlight as their food. Next are the small animals that feed on plants. Then there are the animals that eat them.

After that, there is an even larger animal hunting for its food.

harbor seal

killer whale

The hunters are called predators. The victims are called prey.

Different animals feed on different things. So there are thousands of different food chains in the oceans. One is shown here.

phytoplankton

copepods

herring

cod

Nothing is wasted in the oceans. Animal droppings, and dead animals and plants, are broken down by tiny bacteria. This releases minerals. The minerals help to nourish the phytoplankton.

bacteria
(seen through a
powerful microscope)

Ocean power

One day, the ocean might be used as a source of energy.

A power station in Norway uses waves to generate electricity. Waves push seawater up a special channel into a reservoir. The trapped water spins machines called turbines. The turbines generate electricity.

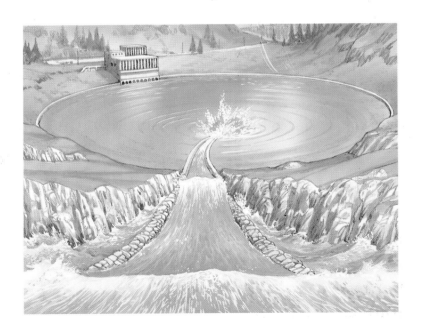

In France, engineers have built a tidal barrage across the mouth of the Rance River. Inside the barrage, turbines generate electricity when they are spun around by seawater. What happens? When the tide goes out, seawater pushes through the turbines and makes them spin. When the tide comes in, the turbines spin the other way.

Scientists and engineers are still experimenting with waves and tides.

More research will have to be done before these ideas work well enough to become useful sources of energy.

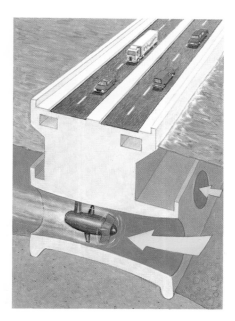

Spoiling the sea

When people dump waste into the sea, they are polluting or dirtying the water.

Pollution harms the plants and animals that live in the sea.

Some factories let poisonous waste flow into rivers and down to the sea. Farm fertilizers and pesticides also seep into the oceans. Many of them harm sea life.

Sometimes the sea is used as a garbage dump. Towns and cities pump sewage through pipelines into the sea. Barges tow garbage out to sea to get rid of it.

Oil spills from tankers can kill thousands of birds and other animals in the sea.

When the oil is washed ashore by tides and currents, it ruins our beaches too. It takes a lot of hard work to clean up the coastline after an oil spill.

🐚 Saving the sea

The oceans are beautiful, and they are valuable. Everyone should do all they can to help protect them.

Conservation groups such as Greenpeace try to protect the oceans. But there is still a lot to do.

What can you do?

You could start by cleaning up your local beach. When you visit the seashore, you could make sure you and your friends do not leave trash behind.

Best of all, you could learn more about the sea. Then you will know how to protect it.

Amazing facts

Ninety-seven percent of all the water on the Earth is in the oceans.

The Pacific Ocean is the biggest ocean and the deepest. The Arctic Ocean is the smallest and the most shallow.

Extra-high tides occur when the Moon is between the Earth and the Sun. Then the Sun and the Moon both pull on the oceans. These tides are called spring tides.

The highest underwater mountain is in the Pacific Ocean, between Samoa and New Zealand. It is 28,480 feet high. That is nearly as tall as Mount Everest, the world's highest mountain.

Plants

🍃 All different

Plants come in all shapes and sizes. Look at the difference between tiny duckweed . . .

duckweed

. . . and a huge tree with branches, roots, and a thick trunk! Or a daffodil with long leaves and a round bulb, and a fern with no flowers.

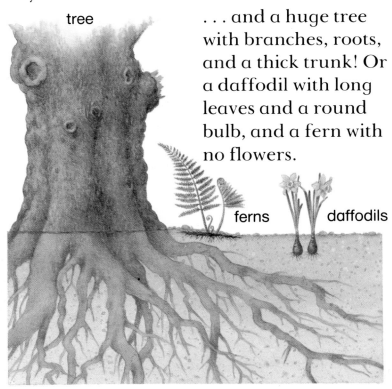
tree

ferns

daffodils

Some plants do not
have roots in soil.
Epiphyte is the name
for any plant that
grows perched on
other plants. This
epiphyte is growing
on a tree.

Brightly colored
bellflowers grow
between the stones
of a wall.

Palm trees have no
branches. Marks on
the trunks show
where the old, dead
leaves have fallen off.

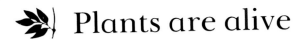

Plants are alive

Like all living things, plants need food to give them energy. Plants make their own food. Their roots take water from the soil, and their leaves take a gas called carbon dioxide from the air.

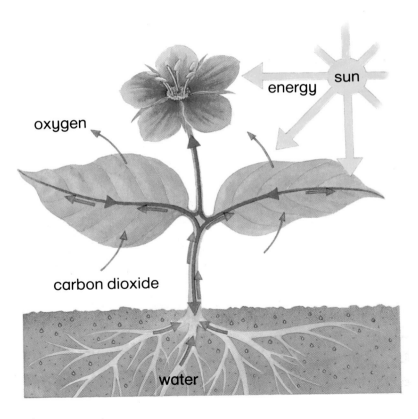

oxygen

sun

energy

carbon dioxide

water

The water travels up the stem to the leaves, which contain a green chemical called chlorophyll. The chlorophyll uses carbon dioxide and sunlight to change the water from the roots into sugar. This process is called photosynthesis. The sugar feeds the whole plant.

Plants give off another gas, called oxygen, during photosynthesis. Plants use some of this oxygen for breathing, just as people and animals do. Plants sweat too. Some of the water soaked up by the roots is given off by the leaves. You can see this water inside a greenhouse or a bell jar.

Plants can adapt

Many plants live in very difficult environments, or surroundings. Very slowly, over thousands of years, they change to suit their environments. The changes are called adaptation.

The saguaro cactus stores water in its thick stems, to survive in the desert.

The water crowfoot has two kinds of leaves. Under the water, finely divided leaves let water flow through easily. On the surface, bigger leaves catch the sunlight.

Gunnera leaves are very large, up to 10 feet across, so they catch a lot of sunlight for photosynthesis.

The little leaves of the dwarf hebe are thick and juicy, because they store water.

Reproduction

Many plants have flowers. Flowers make the seeds that grow new plants. Each flower has male parts, the stamens, and female parts, the pistils. Petals protect these parts.

If you look closely, you'll see that the center of a sunflower has many small flowers.

stigma
(part of
the pistil)

sunflower

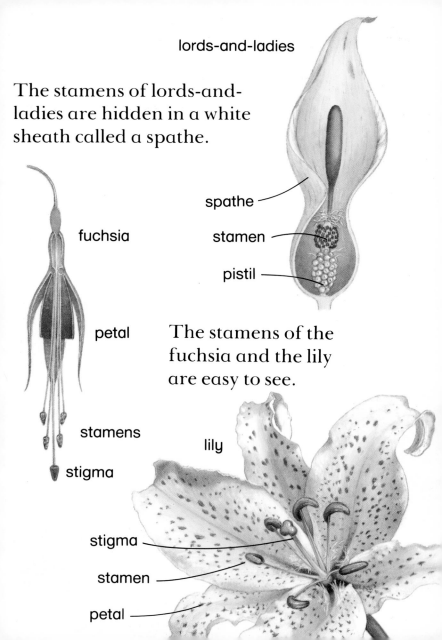

lords-and-ladies

The stamens of lords-and-ladies are hidden in a white sheath called a spathe.

fuchsia

spathe

stamen

pistil

petal

The stamens of the fuchsia and the lily are easy to see.

stamens

stigma

lily

stigma

stamen

petal

 Pollen

A flower's stamens produce tiny grains of pollen. The pistil contains eggs called ovules. For a plant to make seeds, the pollen has to reach the ovules. This is called pollination. It takes place in several ways.

Pine trees make pollen in little yellow cones instead of flowers. The wind blows the pollen to ovules, which are in red cones.

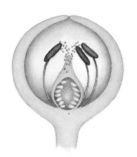

In some flowers, pollination takes place between the stamens and pistil of the same flower, before it opens. This is known as self-pollination.

Animals help to pollinate flowers. This bee is attracted by the bright color and sweet smell of the dog rose. Pollen sticks to the bee's furry body on one flower, and brushes off on another flower.

Many flowers also have a sweet liquid called nectar that attracts bees and other insects.

101

🌿 From flower to fruit

After the pollen becomes attached to the pistil and reaches the ovules inside, the eggs produce seeds. A fruit develops around the seed, sometimes around several seeds. The petals begin to drop off.

Rose hips are the fruits of the dog rose. They contain lots of small seeds.

Pears contain seeds called pips.

The pumpkin plant has male and female flowers. After pollination, the female flower grows a fruit called a berry.

The berry grows into a big pumpkin, containing lots of seeds.

 # Seeds

The fruit protects the seeds while they grow.

Some fruits contain a single seed inside a hard pit. Other fruits have several seeds, called pips, in their juicy pulp.

FRUITS WITH PITS

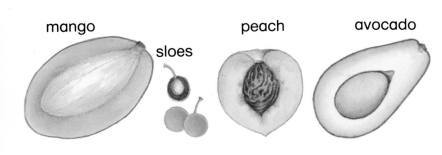

mango

sloes

peach

avocado

FRUITS WITH PIPS

pomegranate

kiwi fruit

bilberries

passion fruit

A strawberry has
lots of pips. Each
pip contains
one seed.

Calabashes, or bottle
gourds, are large,
tough fruits that are
used to hold
water in Africa.

Nuts are one-
seeded fruits
covered by a hard
shell.

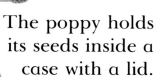

The poppy holds
its seeds inside a
case with a lid.

105

Germination

When seeds are buried in soil and watered, they begin to swell. A baby plant bursts out of each one. This is called germination.

Here is the germination of a fava bean. The bean is a seed. A small root appears first and grows downward. Then the leafy shoot pushes up into the light.

Some seeds send up one or two leaves called seed leaves, or cotyledons, before the shoot appears. But the fava bean's seed leaves stay underground, in the seed.

Fava beans are delicious. But beans from the pod can also be used to grow new plants.

The gardener makes a trench in the soil, puts in the beans, and covers them. Then she waters the soil.

In warm weather, the beans take just a few days to germinate.

Plants without seeds

The whole process of growing new plants is called reproduction. But not all plants reproduce with seeds. Some use their roots, others use their bulbs or stems.

The tulip grows a new plant from a bulb.

The iris grows new plants from its underground stem every year. The stem is called a rhizome.

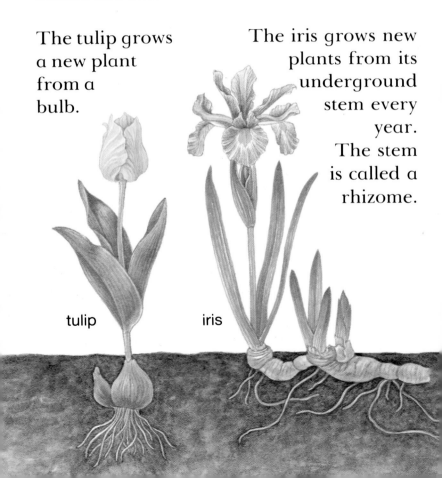

tulip

iris

onion

The layers of an onion bulb are the young stem and leaves.

cassava

The strawberry plant sends out runners, which take root and produce new plants.

strawberry

The cassava plant sprouts up from tubers.

Tubers are underground stems full of food.

Clever plants

Plants develop weapons to protect themselves. They can repel animals and people who threaten their lives.

The nettle has hairs that sting.

The fly agaric is poisonous.

Do not touch!

Rose thorns prick.

Holly scratches.

So does the cactus.

Some plants need
insects to help them
produce new plants.
They attract
the insects
with smells.
(You can find out
how insects help
plants on page 101.)

The rafflesia has a
smell of rotting meat
that attracts flies.

Lilacs give off a
sweeter, nicer
scent!

The flower of the
bee orchid looks
and smells like a
bee. So real bees
sometimes come to
investigate.

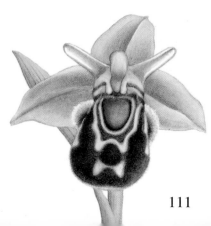

Plants for life

Plants are an essential part of life.

- Plants use energy from the Sun to grow.
- Plants are food for animals.
- Animal droppings and the remains of dead plants and animals are taken into the soil by insects and worms.
- Soil provides some food for plants.

The panda depends on bamboo, because it eats little else.

Trees are
habitats.
That means
they are homes
for other plants
and animals.

One oak tree
may have 400
species living
on it.

Amazing facts

Bamboo is the fastest growing plant in the world. It can grow as much as 3 feet a day.

Giant sequoia trees are over 2,600 feet high. The biggest weigh over 6,000 tons. These trees are the largest living things ever.

The "eyes" of a potato are really small buds that grow leafy shoots if the potato is planted.

At least 400 species of plants become extinct (die out forever) every year.

Dinosaurs

🦕 Meeting dinosaurs

You can see all kinds of dinosaurs in a museum. But no one has ever seen one alive. Museum dinosaurs are models and skeletons.

The real dinosaurs lived millions of years ago. Then they became extinct. That means they died out, forever.

Deinonychus model

model of Tyrannosaurus rex's head

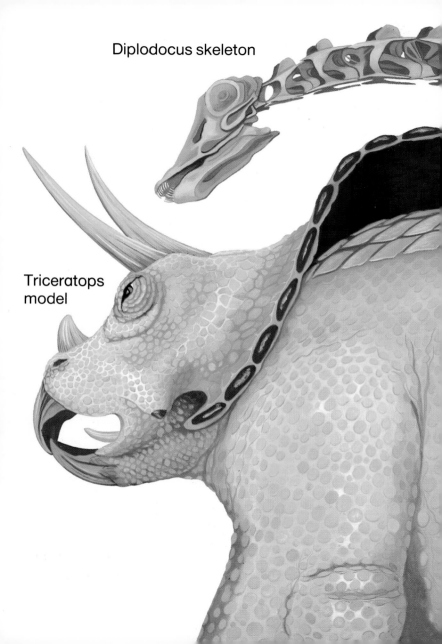

Diplodocus skeleton

Triceratops model

Dinosaur clues

We know about dinosaurs mainly from their bones. But there are other clues. They all help scientists to work out what dinosaurs looked like and how they lived.

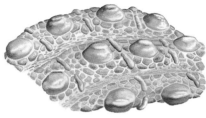

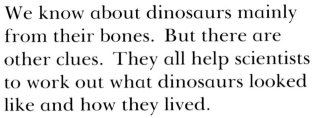

Sometimes prints of dinosaur skin are found. The prints were made in soft mud millions of years ago. The mud has hardened into rock.

Iguanodon model, 1853

New discoveries change our ideas about what dinosaurs looked like.

Teeth and claws tell us what dinosaurs ate. Footprints show the shape of the foot, and even how fast the dinosaur ran.

Some of the rarest finds are dinosaur eggs and nests. Sometimes a baby's skeleton is still inside.

In 1853, people thought Iguanodon had a horn on its nose. Now we know the horn was a spike on its thumb.

now

Big and small

Some dinosaurs were huge. Seismosaurus was the biggest. If it were alive today, and you stood at the end of its tail, you could hardly see to the top of its head. Its name means "earth-shaker," and it probably weighed up to 90 tons!

Diplodocus

Diplodocus was one of the longest dinosaurs—100 feet long! That is about the same length as three buses bumper to bumper.

Compsognathus

Seismosaurus

Brachiosaurus

Big Brachiosaurus
ate only plants.
So did Diplodocus
and Seismosaurus.

Tyrannosaurus rex

Compsognathus

Tyrannosaurus rex ate other animals.
This monster was the biggest meat-eater
ever. Compsognathus was a meat-eater
too. But it was only the size of a turkey.

Plant-eaters

Most dinosaurs were herbivores, which means they ate plants. There was no grass then, but there were many kinds of leaves, fruits, roots, and cones to feed on.

Edmontosaurus and the other duck-bills were plant-eaters.

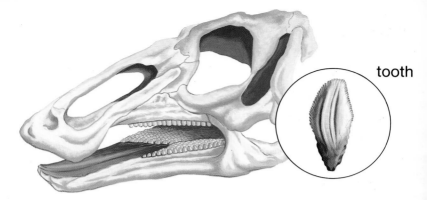

tooth

Edmontosaurus' skull had a wide bony beak at the front, for nipping bits off a plant. Dozens, even hundreds, of teeth lined the jaws near the back. These were used for chewing and grinding the food.

Edmontosaurus' teeth were worn down by all the chewing and grinding. So new teeth were always growing.

Some plant-eaters swallowed pebbles, just as birds swallow grit, to help grind up the food in their stomachs. Scientists call them stomach stones.

Meat-eaters

Some dinosaurs were carnivores, which means they ate meat. Small meat-eaters fed on lizards, frogs, and other small animals. Others were big enough to feed on other dinosaurs.

Meat-eaters had strong jaws. Their teeth were pointed and curved backward, good for tearing flesh. The edges had sharp zig-zags, like the blade of a steak knife.

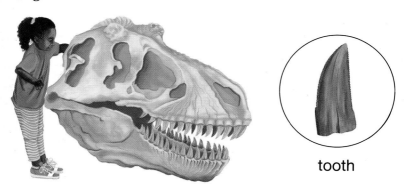

tooth

The biggest meat-eater was Tyrannosaurus rex. It could have swallowed you in a couple of mouthfuls!

🦕 Dinosaur defenses

Plant-eaters had to defend themselves
from the meat-eaters.

Triceratops

Triceratops had
three horns for
fighting off a
meat-eater. And
a large bony
shield protected
its neck from
attack.

Iguanodon had two
sharp thumb spikes.
A nasty stab from
one of those
would scare off
the enemy!

Iguanodon

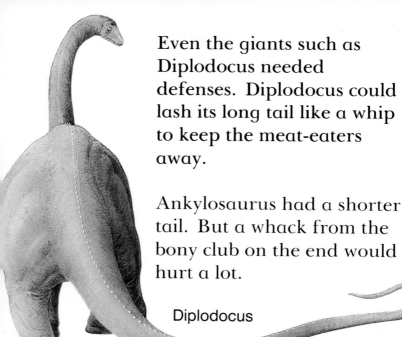

Even the giants such as Diplodocus needed defenses. Diplodocus could lash its long tail like a whip to keep the meat-eaters away.

Ankylosaurus had a shorter tail. But a whack from the bony club on the end would hurt a lot.

Diplodocus

Ankylosaurus also had bony armor over its back and head. So this big plant-eater was safe from most meat-eaters.

Ankylosaurus

🦕 Clever or stupid?

People used to think that dinosaurs were not very clever. This was because dinosaur skulls have only a small space for a brain.

Stegosaurus weighed six or seven tons, so it was as heavy as an elephant. But it had a brain the size of a walnut.

Perhaps Stegosaurus did not need a big brain. After all, it was big and safe from most attackers, and it spent most of the day grazing slowly.

brain

Other dinosaurs had bigger brains.

Stenonychosaurus was a fast little meat-eater. It had big eyes and a good sense of smell for finding small animals to eat. It had long, strong fingers for grabbing them too. Because Stenonychosaurus was a hunter, it needed a bigger brain.

Hot or cold?

Stegosaurus

Reptiles are cold-blooded. Dinosaurs were reptiles, so were they cold-blooded? Scientists are not sure.

Cold-blooded animals do not make heat inside their bodies. If the air around them is warm, they are warm and active. If the air is cold, they are cold and sluggish. Warm-blooded animals stay warm and active even if the air is cold, because their bodies *do* make heat.

Perhaps Stegosaurus was cold-blooded. Perhaps the plates on its back soaked up the sun's heat in the morning, and lost heat if it got too warm later on.

But maybe big, slow dinosaurs were too big to change temperature and were warm-blooded.

Diplodocus

Maybe small, active dinosaurs were warm-blooded too.

Deinonychus

131

What happened?

The death of the dinosaurs has always been a mystery. Ever since dinosaur bones were first discovered, people all over the world have tried to solve the mystery.

Some of the ideas or theories seem funny.
Some theories seem more likely.
But no one knows for certain which theory is right.

Perhaps dinosaurs were too stupid to survive. But if that were true, why did they live so long?

Perhaps mammals ate too many of their eggs. But why didn't this happen earlier?

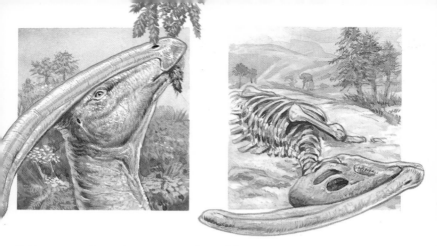

Many scientists wonder if the climate
became cooler all over the Earth. Perhaps
dinosaurs could not live without warmth.

Perhaps new plants
poisoned the
dinosaurs. But
there were other
plants to eat.

Perhaps they were too
big. But the smaller ones
disappeared too.

133

A big bang

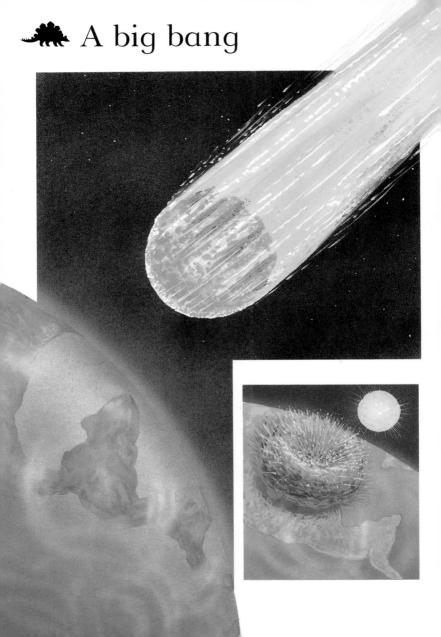

Perhaps the dinosaurs were killed by an enormous asteroid. An asteroid is a rock that hurtles through space. It may be hundreds of miles across.

Sixty-five million years ago a meteorite miles wide hit the Earth. This is what might have happened next...

The crash threw up a huge cloud of dust, high into the sky. The dust blocked out the sun. With no sunlight, the air became cold and plants died. The dinosaurs perished.

The dinosaur hunters

People have known about dinosaurs for less than 200 years. Huge bones were dug up in quarries, but no one knew what they were. Were they the bones of elephants, or dragons, or giants?

In 1822 Georges Cuvier suggested that the bones might belong to giant reptiles.

Georges Cuvier

"reptiles"

William Buckland

Gideon & Mary Mantell

William Buckland was the first person to name a dinosaur. In 1824 he named Megalosaurus, meaning "big lizard."

Gideon and Mary Mantell were keen fossil hunters. In 1825, Gideon named a second dinosaur, Iguanodon.

In 1842, Richard Owen invented the word dinosaurs, or "terrible lizards."

More dinosaurs were discovered in North America—Othniel Marsh and Edward Cope found dozens from 1870 to 1900.

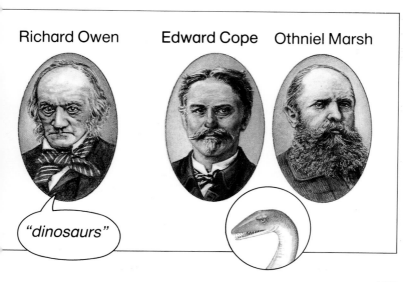

Richard Owen   Edward Cope   Othniel Marsh

"dinosaurs"

Amazing facts

The oldest dinosaur we know was named Eoraptor in 1993. It lived about 225 million years ago. It was only three feet long, but it was a fierce meat-eater.

Dinosaur footprints were first found around 1800 in North America. People thought they were made by giant birds. Now we know they belonged to a dinosaur called Anchiosaurus.

Every year, about ten new species of dinosaurs are named. They come from all over the world.

Some scientists think that asteroids, like the one that may have killed the dinosaurs, hit the Earth every 26 million years. If so, the next one is due in 13 million years.

Animals

🐾 Animal groups

There are many different kinds of animals.
Scientists arrange them in groups.

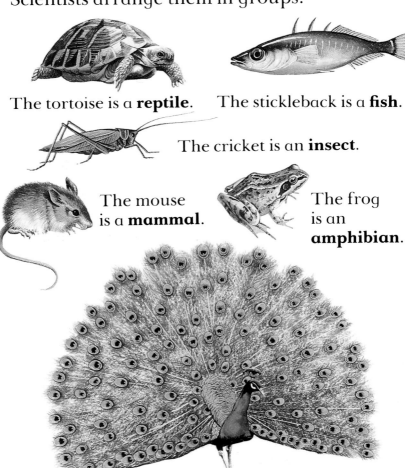

The tortoise is a **reptile**.   The stickleback is a **fish**.

The cricket is an **insect**.

The mouse
is a **mammal**.

The frog
is an
amphibian.

The peacock is a **bird**.

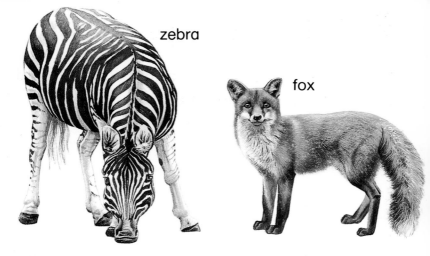

zebra

fox

All the members of a group have similar features. The animals on this page are all mammals. They are more closely related to each other than to birds or reptiles or fish.

panda

brown bear

☙ How many animals?

There are over 1 million kinds, or species, of animals. Each one is different.

Scientists divide all the species into two main groups. The animals with backbones are called vertebrates. The animals without backbones are called invertebrates.

The two main groups are divided into smaller groups. You can find out about these groups in the rest of this book.

Some species are dying out because their homes and their food supplies are destroyed when people cut down forests, drain marshes, or pollute rivers and seas.

4,000 amphibians   4,150 mammals   6,500 reptiles

    VERTEBRATES

This chart shows you how many species there are in each group.

8,800 birds   21,500 fish   A million others

INVERTEBRATES

✤ Worms

Earthworms belong to a group of animals called annelids. They have no eyes, ears, or legs.

Earthworms spend their lives under the ground, tunneling. Tiny bristles help them grip the soil as they wriggle along.

Earthworms swallow soil while they make
their tunnels. They digest the dead plants
that are in the soil and push the rest
up above ground. These small heaps
of leftovers are called worm casts.

worm cast

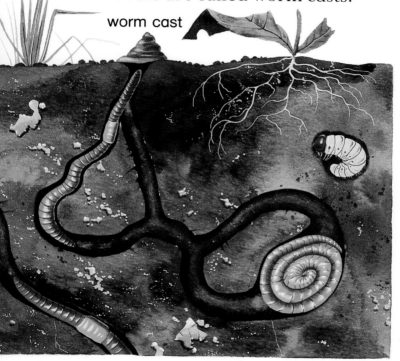

At night, earthworms come to the surface to
look for dead leaves. They pull the leaves
into their burrows to eat there in safety.

❧ Insects

Insects have six legs, and most insects can fly. Some insects have one pair of wings; some have two pairs.

This ladybug has two pairs of wings. The front wings are hard, and they cover the delicate back wings when the ladybug is not flying.

Every insect's body has three parts: a head at the front, a thorax in the middle and an abdomen at the back.

Other insects include ants, bees, flies, butterflies, and grasshoppers.

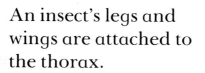

An insect's legs and wings are attached to the thorax.

Insects have two eyes and can see all around.

They also have two antennae to help them feel and smell things.

eye

antenna

Ladybugs feed on tiny insects called aphids.

aphid

Some insects have mouths that suck like straws. But ladybugs have jaws for biting.

✤ Spiders

Spiders have eight legs. They belong to a group of animals called arachnids.

Spiders build webs with silk. They pull threads of silk from tiny spinnerets.

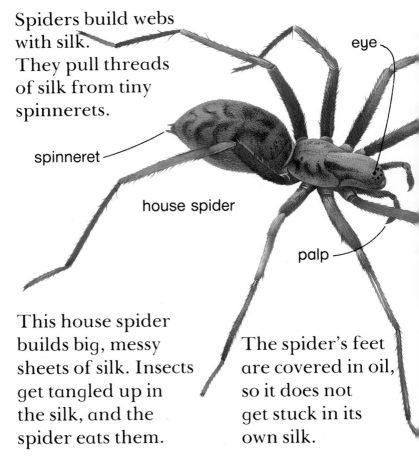

eye

spinneret

house spider

palp

This house spider builds big, messy sheets of silk. Insects get tangled up in the silk, and the spider eats them.

The spider's feet are covered in oil, so it does not get stuck in its own silk.

Many spiders can walk up walls and across ceilings because their feet have hairy pads for extra grip.

The biggest spiders are the bird-eating spiders. Some of them measure 10 inches across — big enough to cover a dinner plate.

Most spiders have two rows of four eyes — that's eight eyes altogether.

But spiders don't see very well. They have sensitive hairs on their legs and two feelers, called palps, to help them find their way around.

As they get bigger, spiders grow new skins and shed their old ones.

 # Fish

A fish spends its whole life in water. Some fish live in the sea, some in rivers and lakes. Their bodies are usually covered with scales.

Scales grow bigger each year. So, they can show how old a fish is.

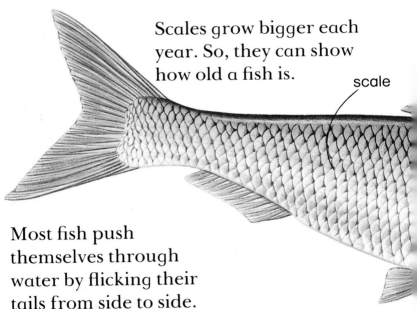

scale

Most fish push themselves through water by flicking their tails from side to side.

eggs

Fish steer themselves with their fins. They also use their fins as brakes, to slow down.

Like all animals, fish need oxygen to live. We get our oxygen from the air we breathe, but fish get theirs from water.

Water enters the fish's mouth and passes over its gills, which absorb the oxygen. Then the water goes out through gill slits at the side of the head.

fin

Fish have no eyelids, so their eyes are always open.

gill slits

herring

Most fish lay eggs. This herring lays thousands of eggs at a time. The eggs have no shells, and many are eaten by other fish. Only a few hatch into babies.

🐾 Amphibians

Frogs, toads, newts, and salamanders are all amphibians. An amphibian begins its life as an egg laid in water. A tadpole hatches from the egg. When the tadpole turns into an adult, it leaves the water.

Amphibians cannot live in salt water, so there are none in the sea.

Frogs and toads have long, powerful back legs for jumping and swimming.

They use their webbed feet like paddles in the water.

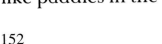

Amphibians have two big eyes at the top of their head, so they can see all around.
They have a good sense of smell, too, even under water.

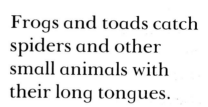

Frogs and toads catch spiders and other small animals with their long tongues.

European green toad

Like reptiles, amphibians are cold-blooded animals. But they have soft, moist skin without scales.

 Reptiles

Crocodiles, snakes, lizards, tortoises, and turtles are all reptiles. Dinosaurs, which lived long ago, were reptiles too.

Reptiles have scaly skin. Many of them are brightly colored, like this lizard.

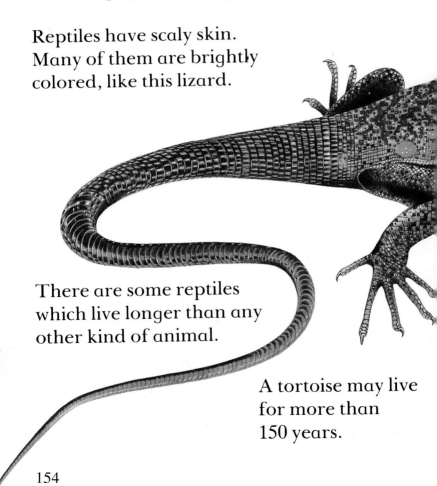

There are some reptiles which live longer than any other kind of animal.

A tortoise may live for more than 150 years.

Reptiles are cold-blooded animals. This means that they cannot keep their bodies warm in cold weather. They need lots of sunshine to keep warm. That is why most reptiles live in hot countries.

If they get too hot, they hurry into the shade or into some cool water.

ocellated lizard

Some reptiles give birth to live young, but most lay eggs. Their eggs are not hard like birds' eggs, but soft and leathery.

Reptiles that live in cold countries hibernate during the winter and wake up in the spring.

 Birds

All birds have feathers and wings, and most birds can fly.

pigeon

When a bird
flaps its wings,
the feathers push the air
back and down, so the bird
moves forward and up.

When winter comes, some birds fly thousands of miles to find warmer countries. This is called migration.

All birds lay eggs.
A baby hatches out of the egg by cracking the shell.

A bird's eyes are usually on either side of its head. So it can see almost everything around it. It hears well too.

Birds have no teeth. Instead, they have a hard beak or bill.

Birds have two feet, with claws for gripping.

Mammals

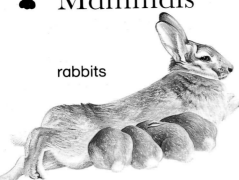

rabbits

Mammal babies feed on milk from their mother's body.

All mammals have hair on their bodies. Some have a thick furry coat to keep them warm in cold weather.

We are mammals too.

Most mammals live on land and move on four legs.

Some mammals hunt other animals for food. These meat-eaters are called carnivores.

Others, such as this rabbit, are herbivores — they eat only plants.

Mammals can hear and see and smell things around them.

Dogs, cats, monkeys, and whales are mammals.

Some mammals use their fingers and toes to grasp things.

Amazing facts

🐾 The biggest animal of all is the blue whale. Blue whales are as long as six elephants. The heaviest one weighed 190 tons.

🐾 The slowest mammal is the sloth, which spends its life hanging upside down in the trees of South American forests. It never moves faster than about half a mile per hour.

🐾 Every year the Arctic tern flies across the world, from the Arctic to the Antarctic and back again. That's about 24,800 miles.

🐾 Lizards can snap off their tails when they are attacked. The attacker is left with just the tail, and the lizard escapes. Then the lizard grows a new tail.

My Body

✺ Where do you come from

The body is made of millions of tiny living parts called cells – bone cells and skin cells, brain cells and blood cells, cells for every part of your body.

But we all began as just one cell inside our mother's body, before we were born. Every baby is made by a man and a woman. They are the baby's parents.

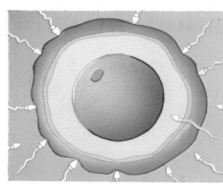

A sperm from the father enters an egg inside the mother.

Now the egg is fertilized. It is the first cell of the baby.

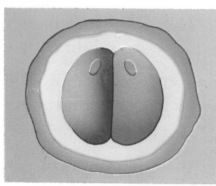

The egg is even smaller than a dot made by a pencil.

The egg splits into two cells, and then into four, and so on.

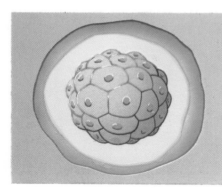

So the egg grows bigger and bigger.

The egg moves to a part of the mother called the womb. This is the start of her pregnancy.

✗ Nine months for a baby

The baby grows in a bag of warm liquid in the mother's womb. It gets all the food and oxygen it needs from its mother's body, through a tube called the umbilical cord.

At one month, the baby's heart is beating. The baby is no bigger than a pea.

At three months, it is about 2½ inches long and looks more like a baby.

At four months, it can move around.

At five months, it sucks its thumb.

At six months, it can hear sounds.

At nine months, the baby is ready to come out of its mother's womb.

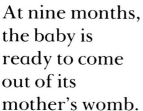

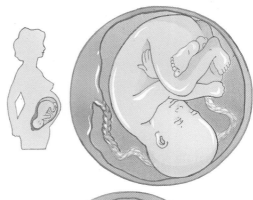

Then it usually turns upside down.

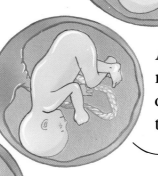

At eight months, it can taste things.

At seven months, it opens its eyes. It can kick strongly.

165

✗ Hair and nails

We have hair all over our bodies, except for our palms and the soles of our feet.

You see only part of the hair. The rest is under the skin. It is called the root. When you are cold, a little muscle pulls the hair upright. You have goose pimples!

normal hair

hair standing   on end

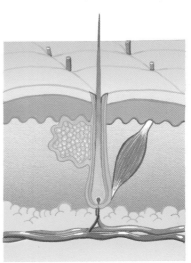

skin

root   muscle

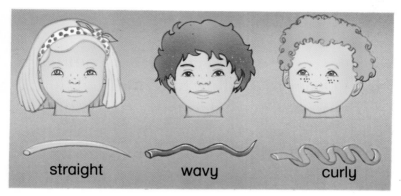

straight   wavy   curly

Hair grows out of tiny holes in our skin. Some people's hair grows straight, some wavy, and some curly.

Hair is made of keratin. So are our nails. Nails protect our toes and fingertips.

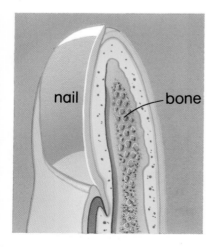

nail —— bone

A cat's claws are its nails.

✘ Teeth

We bite into food and chew it with our teeth so it is easier to swallow and digest. The sharp incisors at the front are for cutting. Pointed canines at the sides are for tearing. Big molars at the back are for crushing.

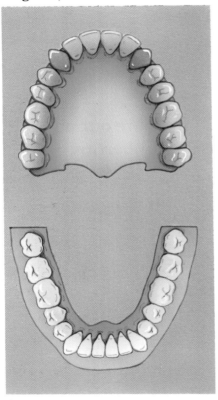

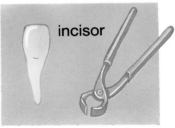

incisor

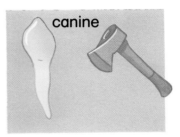

canine

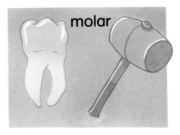

molar

A hard layer of enamel covers the dentin. Inside this is the pulp, the sensitive part. Under the gum, each tooth has a root that holds it in place in the jaw bone.

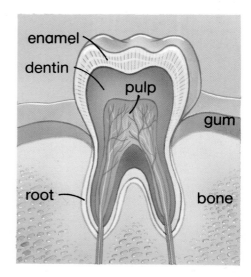

enamel
dentin
pulp
gum
root
bone

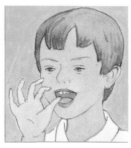

When we are about six years old, our first teeth become loose and fall out.

They make room for the larger teeth that are growing underneath.

 # Muscles

Under our skin are the muscles. We use muscles whenever we move.

Muscles are joined to bones. They contract, or tighten, to pull a bone, and relax, or loosen, to release it.

We have more than 650 muscles in our bodies. They move every part of the body, not just bones. The muscles in our face help us to smile, frown, wink, and chew. The muscles in our chest help us to breathe.

Muscles grow bigger and stronger with exercise and training.

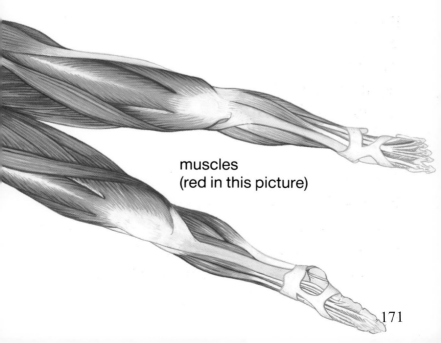

muscles
(red in this picture)

✗ The skeleton

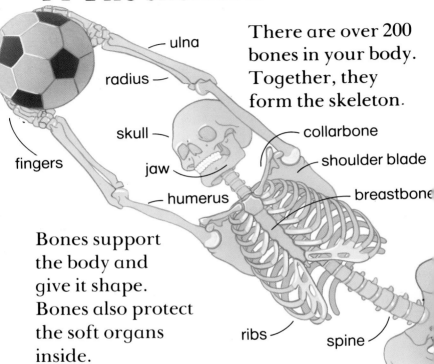

ulna

radius

skull

jaw

humerus

fingers

collarbone

shoulder blade

breastbone

ribs

spine

There are over 200 bones in your body. Together, they form the skeleton.

Bones support the body and give it shape. Bones also protect the soft organs inside.

Your nose feels hard, but it is not all bone. The tip of it is a delicate piece of cartilage or gristle.

As you grow up,
your bones grow
longer and
thicker. So you
grow taller and
heavier too.

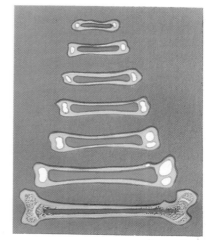

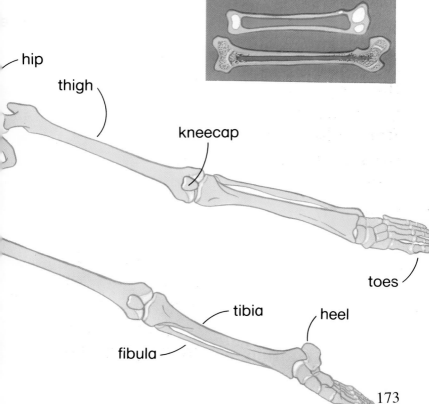

hip

thigh

kneecap

toes

tibia

heel

fibula

173

✗ The brain

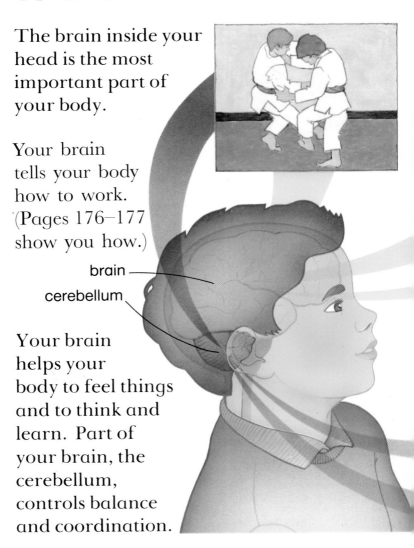

The brain inside your head is the most important part of your body.

Your brain tells your body how to work. (Pages 176–177 show you how.)

brain

cerebellum

Your brain helps your body to feel things and to think and learn. Part of your brain, the cerebellum, controls balance and coordination.

The nervous system

A network of nerves links every part of the body with the brain.

From our senses, the nerves receive information about our bodies and the world around us.

The nerves send the information as electric signals to the spinal cord. This is a thick bundle of nerves down the middle of our backs. The spinal cord carries the signals up to the brain.

The brain sorts out the information. It sends commands along other nerves to tell the body's organs and muscles how to react.

All of this happens very quickly, in less than a second.

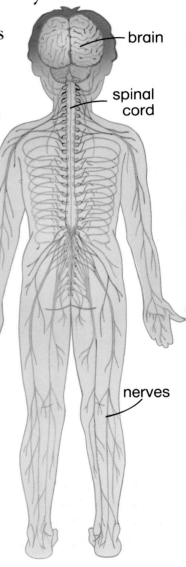

brain

spinal cord

nerves

Our nervous system helps us to use
our senses, to think, remember and
plan, and to move.

Sometimes we do things without thinking.
When you touch something sharp, your hand
will jerk away, without waiting for a message
from the brain. This is called reflex action.

✗ Other organs

The brain is one of the soft organs inside your body. The other organs all have special tasks of their own. They help the body to work properly.

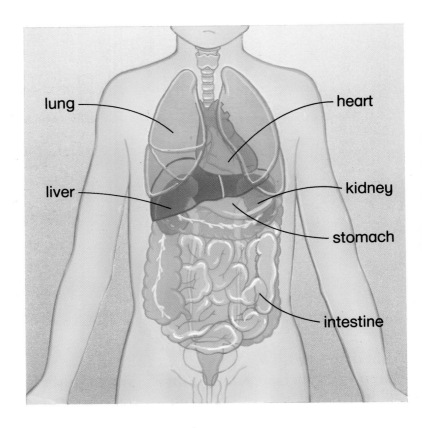

lung

heart

liver

kidney

stomach

intestine

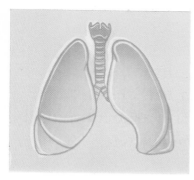

The lungs supply blood with oxygen.

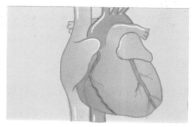

The heart pumps blood around the body.

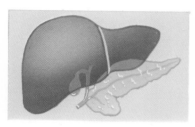

The liver helps us to digest our food.

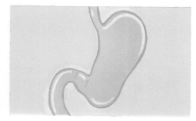

The stomach mashes food into a pulp.

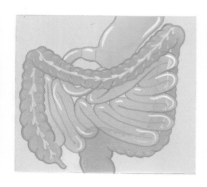

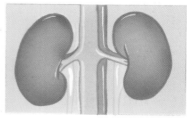

◄ The intestines pass food into the blood.

▲ Two kidneys help to get rid of waste.

✗ Breathing

We need oxygen to stay alive. Our lungs take oxygen from the air we breathe. Our blood takes the oxygen from the lungs and carries it to the rest of the body.

It is impossible to stay underwater without a snorkel or air tanks, because there is no air to breathe.

When you breathe in through your nose or your mouth, air goes down your windpipe and into your lungs.

Blood travels through your lungs and collects oxygen from them. Blood also carries used air back to the lungs.

When you breathe out, your lungs push the used air back out through your nose or your mouth.

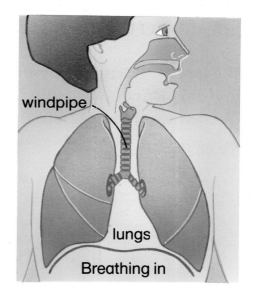

windpipe

lungs

Breathing in

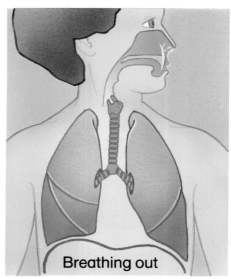

Breathing out

✕ Hearing

We hear sounds all the time. They are invisible waves in the air. Some sounds are pleasant, some are not. But they all give us information about the world around us.

We can see only part of the ear. The rest is inside the head. Sounds enter the ear and make the eardrum vibrate. This makes tiny bones move. Then a nerve carries the message to the brain.

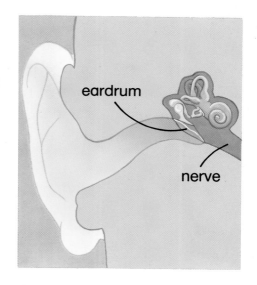

The brain tells us what we are hearing.

A hearing aid makes sounds louder, to help people who cannot hear well.

✗ Smell

We use the nose for breathing and for smelling. Smells float in the air. Although they are invisible, we can tell what they are. We like some smells, but not others!

When a smell reaches the back of your nose, nerves carry the information to the brain. The brain decides what the smell is.

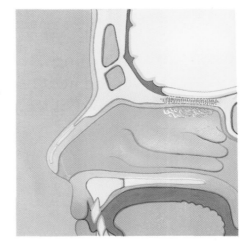

Some doctors look after only the ears, nose, and throat.

Our sense of smell helps our sense of taste. That is why it is difficult to taste things when you have a cold and a stuffed nose.

✗ Touch

When we touch things, we can feel them.
Our skin feels the heat of a cup of hot
chocolate, the cold of ice, the prick of a
thorn, the softness of a cat's fur.

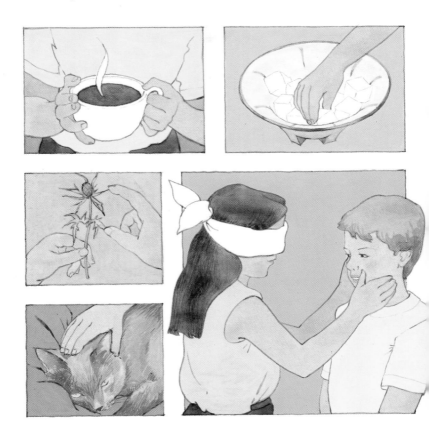

Tiny nerves in the skin send messages to the brain about things we touch.

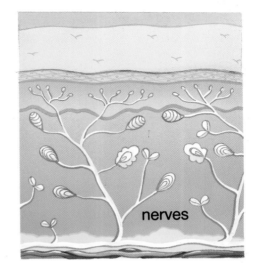

nerves

reading in braille

A blind person can read and write braille, by using her sense of touch.

writing in braille

The pianist controls the pressure of his fingers on the keys to play loudly or softly.

✘ Taste

The tongue feels heat, cold, pain, and different tastes.

sweet

salty

All over your tongue are thousands of little bumps called taste buds. Inside the buds are nerves that send messages to the brain about what you are eating.

There are four types of taste: sweet, salty, bitter, and sour. The tongue has areas which are especially good at recognizing each one of these tastes.

The best way to taste ice cream is to lick it with the tip of your tongue, which is the best part for picking up sweet tastes.

sour

bitter

The back of the tongue recognizes bitter tastes.

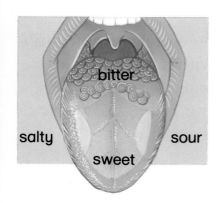

The sides recognize sour and salty tastes.

The front recognizes sweet tastes.

189

✖ Sight

We see the world around us with our eyes. They help us to recognize shape, height, distance, and color.

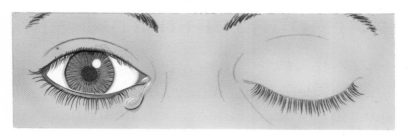

Every time you blink, your eyelids spread
tears over your eyes, to keep them moist
and clean.

The eye is shaped like a ball. It has muscles
attached to it, so it can move up and down and
side to side.

Light bounces off
the things you
look at and enters
your eye through
the pupil. Nerves
in the retina send
messages to the
brain. The brain
tells you what
you see.

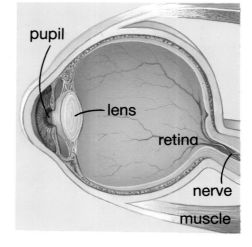

pupil

lens

retina

nerve

muscle

✘ Eating for energy

We eat food because it gives our bodies energy. People eat many kinds of food, but our bodies digest everything in the same way.

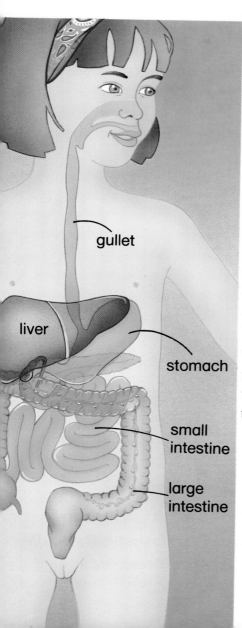

When you swallow food, it moves down a tube into the stomach. The stomach mashes it into pulp. Next, it is squeezed along your intestines.

Now the food is digested, and it passes through the intestine into the blood. The blood takes it around your body.

The body gets rid of the food it cannot use when we go to the bathroom.

gullet

liver

stomach

small intestine

large intestine

✗ When you are ill

When we are ill, we may have a high temperature, a cough, a rash, or aches and pains. These are signs that the body is being attacked by germs.

When the body is fighting off invading germs, it works harder and the heart beats faster. The body's temperature rises.

The doctor examines you to find out which part of you the germs are attacking. She listens to your heart and lungs with a stethoscope, looks in your ears and throat, and asks you questions. Then the doctor decides if you need anything to help you get better.

You may need medicine to fight against the germs.

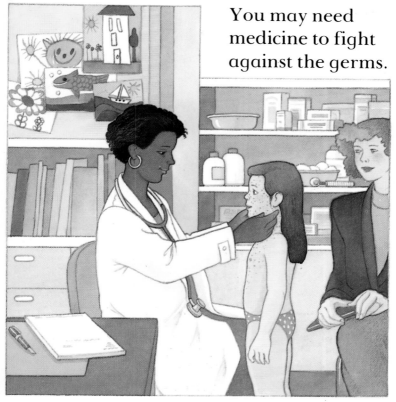

Amazing facts

✗ We all started out as just one cell, but an adult body has about 50 trillion cells.

✗ You take about 23,000 breaths each day.

✗ When you sneeze, air rushes out of your nose at almost 100 miles per hour.

✗ The oldest person ever lived to be 121.

People
Long Ago

The first people

Human beings gradually grew taller

The first people appeared about two million
years ago. They did not wear any clothes
and lived in small groups. Some lived in
caves, while others lived in
simple shelters.

The first humans learned how to make fire and how to make simple tools out of stone. They used these tools to hunt animals and to chop their food.

tools used by
the first people

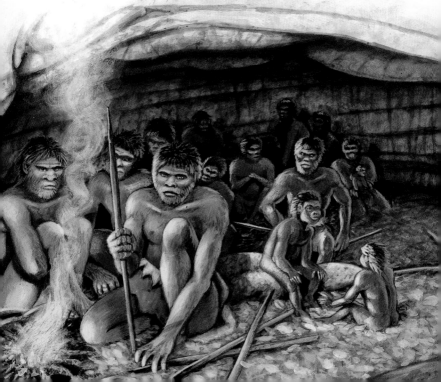

🏛 Pharaohs and gods

Some Egyptian gods

Horus   Isis   Osiris   Ra   Anubis

Most of Egypt is desert, but one of the
greatest rivers in the world, the Nile, runs
through it. Once a year, the Nile flooded
its banks, leaving behind rich soil. Here
the Egyptians settled. Their empire
lasted almost 3,000 years.

The Egyptians believed in many gods.
They also believed that their ruler, the
pharaoh, was a god. When he died,
he was buried with piles of treasure
in a huge pyramid.

pyramid

📜 Life in Rome

About 1,800 years ago, the city of Rome was the center of the biggest empire ever.

In the center of the city was an open area called the Forum. The Forum was ringed by monuments: temples, statues, columns, and splendid arches. Here, the citizens of Rome met to chat and to do business.

A slave helped a noble boy wash and dress.

At school he wrote his lessons on wax tablets.

Afterward he could play with a hoop or knuckle-bones.

In the afternoon he might go to the public baths with his father.

The Vikings

In the cold lands of the north lived the
Vikings. Most Vikings were farmers, but they
were also fierce warriors who raided the
coasts of Europe. They could row and sail
great distances in their light, flat-bottomed
ships, called longships.

Many Vikings set out in search of new farmland. They settled in France, Ireland, Scotland, and the north of England. The Vikings were also skilled craftsmen and their ships were often decorated with beautiful carvings like this one.

prow of a Viking ship

Castles of stone

In Europe, in the Middle Ages, there were many wars, so landowners called lords lived with their families and soldiers in castles. The first castles were built of wood. Later, they were made of stone with a deep ditch, or moat, all the way around the outside.

The peasants who farmed the lord's land lived in villages nearby. But in times of danger, they came into the castle for protection.

In wartime, soldiers stood
guard in towers spaced
along the castle wall.

An imperial city

Outside Europe, other empires had
developed. Emperors ruled over a great
empire in China. In 1421, the emperor
moved his court to the city of Beijing.
He lived with his family and thousands of
servants in a walled palace as big as a town.

The palace was called the Forbidden City, because no one except the emperor's household was allowed inside. In the streets of Beijing, craftsmen wove silk cloth and painted porcelain bowls. China was famous for its silk and porcelain.

⛫ An Aztec city

In America, two great empires had
developed. The Incas lived in what is now
Peru, in South America. In what is now
Mexico, the Aztecs ruled over a great
kingdom from their capital, Tenochtitlán.

Girls prepare incense for a ceremony.

Tenochtitlán was built on islands in the middle of a marshy lake. Canals crisscrossed the city. In the center stood great pyramid-shaped temples where priests performed ceremonies for the Aztec gods.

Priests were often teachers too. Here, a priest teaches children to play musical instruments.

European explorers

Around 550 years ago, European sailors began to explore the world.

caravel

Better sailing ships and new instruments for navigating meant that sailors were able to make longer voyages. Kings and queens encouraged explorers to go and discover new lands and riches. Europeans sailed to Africa, India, the West Indies, and America for the first time.

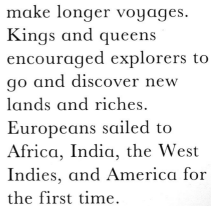

European explorers used new kinds of sailing ships such as the caravel, the carrack, and the nao for their long ocean voyages.

nao

carrack

Settlers in North America

More than 350 years ago, a group of people from England landed in North America to settle there. They were not the first people to live in North America. Tribes of Native Americans had been living there for thousands of years.

The settlers farmed the land and traded with the Native Americans for furs. Over the years their farms grew. Ships filled with wood, tobacco, and sugar from their farms sailed across to Europe.

Although the settlers lived so far away, they were still ruled by the King of England and had to pay him taxes.

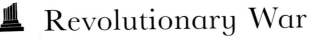 # Revolutionary War

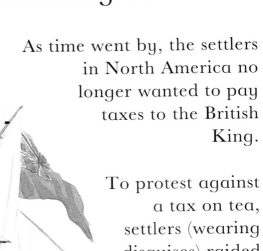

As time went by, the settlers in North America no longer wanted to pay taxes to the British King.

To protest against a tax on tea, settlers (wearing disguises) raided three British ships in Boston harbor and threw their cargo of tea overboard.

This was a signal for other settlers to join a revolt. After six years of fighting, the British were defeated and the settlers became independent. A new country was born; it was called the United States of America. People across the new country celebrated their victory by parading behind their new flag.

Amazing facts

Historians think the first people lived in Africa about two million years ago.

A knight's armor weighed about as much as a ten-year-old child. On top of that, he also had to carry a heavy sword and a shield.

The words avocado, chocolate, and tomato all come from the Náhuatl language. This was the language spoken by the Aztecs more than 500 years ago.

Christopher Columbus sailed to America in 1492. But he believed he had traveled to the East Indies and was somewhere near Japan.

People
and Places

Hello!

jamm nga fënaan

الـ ~ عَلَينكُم

你好嗎

BONJOUR!

تابق

ကို့ဆက်စတာ:॥

नमस्कार

There are about six thousand languages
in the world. Many people speak more
than one language.

Buenos días

ЗДРА́ВСТВУЙ

שָׁלוֹם, בֹּקֶר טוֹב

গুড্ মর্নিং

おはよう

günaydın

καλημέρα

안녕

The words people speak and write may
sound and look very different. Here is how
to say "hello" in just a few languages.

221

Home sweet home

Arctic igloo

Indian tepee

Tuareg tent

Australian house

Borneo
longhouse

Benin
stilt house

cave
dwelling

Irish
cottage

Spanish
hacienda

222

People live in many kinds of homes, built of many kinds of materials, on the ground and on water.

Mongolian yurt

mobile home

Chinese sampan

Marsh Arab straw house

Mali mud house

Southern African hut

Mediterranean house

Venetian palace

skyscraper

223

Religion

Christians believe in one God and in Jesus Christ. They worship in churches.

Jews believe in one God and in the Messiah. The Wailing Wall in Jerusalem is an important place of prayer.

Muslims believe in one God, Allah. Their religion is called Islam. Muslims go on pilgrimage to Mecca.

Hindu pilgrims visit the holy city of Varanasi. Hindus worship many gods, such as Brahma, Shiva, and Vishnu.

Buddhists follow the teachings of Gautama, the Buddha. There are statues of him in Buddhist temples.

Shinto is the ancient religion of Japan. Shinto means "way of the gods" in Japanese. People worship many gods in Shinto shrines.

The frozen north

The far north of Canada is one of the coldest places on Earth. This is where the Inuits live.

Everyone wears warm clothes to keep out the icy cold. Planes bring food and other supplies for the winter.

Sleds pulled by dogs are a good way to get around. But people also drive snowmobiles.

Rubbing noses is the Inuit way of kissing.

This man is fishing through
a hole in the ice. Nearby
is the igloo he has built
for shelter from the cold.
Although the igloo
is made of ice,
it is warm inside.
Inuits use igloos
only when they go
fishing in the winter.

227

A Pueblo festival

Native Americans were the first people to live in America. They still celebrate their ancient festivals. These Pueblo Indians of the United States are dancing to celebrate the Maize Festival.

The dancers wear special costumes and wear corncobs on their heads. They sing to make the rain fall and bring them a good harvest.

228

When Pueblo children play with wooden kachina dolls, they learn about Native American history and legends. Each doll is painted to represent a magical spirit of the earth, sky, or water. This is a winged spirit doll. It represents a spirit of the sky.

This Pueblo medicine man is trying to heal someone who is sick. He draws symbols in the sand. His helpers chant songs.

A town square

It is noon, the hottest part of the day, so the square is almost empty. The people of this small town in Mexico are taking a break from work. They rest in the cool shade under the arches. It is pleasant to eat in the open air—a plate of tasty beans with pancakes called tortillas, or corn roasted on the cob.

Every town has its own fiesta or festival once a year. Then people fill the square.

During the fiesta,
there are fireworks,
music, and dancing.
Children try to break
open a pot called
the piñata, to get
the candy inside.

A city in Europe

Most of the people of Europe live and work in towns and cities. Some European towns are small. Others have grown over many years into big cities.

There are public gardens and parks for everyone to enjoy. Sometimes a band comes to play on the bandstand.

The center of the city is often the business area, with offices, banks, and shops. Side by side, buildings old and new tell the history of the city.

Visitors and townspeople can
have a drink and a meal at
a café in the square.

If the weather is nice, it's fun to sit and
watch the world pass by.

Village life

Villages in Africa can look very different from one another because people use different materials and build in different ways. The houses in this village on the Ivory Coast have thatched roofs.

The people of the village enjoy stories, gossip, and games. Beneath a baobab tree, men are playing a game called awale. The two players move seeds around holes in a block of wood.

The women are preparing a meal together. They pound millet or cassava into flour for baking bread.

Some of the villagers are spinning cotton and weaving it into cloth on a loom.

In Japan

About 120 million people live on the islands of Japan. Indoors, the Japanese take off their shoes. The floor is covered with tatamis, which are mats made of braided rice straw.

At mealtimes, the family kneels around the table.

In the morning, everyone rolls up their futon, or mattress bed, and puts it away.

karate

kendo

judo

The Japanese are known for martial arts.
In kendo, two people fight with staves.
They wear helmets to protect themselves.
In karate and judo,
they fight with
bare hands and
feet. During the
children's festival
on May 5, kites
shaped like fish
fly high in the sky.

carp kites

calligraphy

Schoolchildren
learn calligraphy,
the art of writing
with a brush and
ink on a long
scroll of paper.

👁 Around the world

There are six billion people on Earth, and you are one of them! People around the world speak different languages and have different customs, but they also have many things in common. They all work and play and make friends. We can all help each other and work together to make the world a better place for everybody.

Amazing facts

👁 There are 189 countries in the world. Each country has its own government, flag, capital city, and money.

👁 About 6,000 languages are spoken around the world.

👁 China has more than 1 billion people. That's more than any other country. Next comes India, with about 850 million people.

👁 The city of Venice, Italy, is built on the edge of the sea and has more canals than streets. People often travel in boats instead of cars or buses.

Science

Solids, liquids and gases

All materials are either solids, liquids, or
gases. Solids keep their own shape. They
can be hard, like wood, or soft, like bread.

Liquids take the shape of their container.
If you pour a liquid, it will run. Some liquids
are thick and run more slowly.

Gases won't even stay in their container
unless it is completely sealed. If they escape,
they spread out all over the room.

Materials can turn from solids to
liquids and from liquids to gases.
It often depends on the temperature.
Water comes out of a faucet
as a liquid.

But if we make water
cold enough, it freezes
into a solid—ice.

If we warm ice, it
melts back to water.

If we heat water until
it boils, it turns into
a gas—steam. We
call this change
evaporation.

If we let steam cool, it
turns back into a liquid.
We call this change
condensation.

243

Mixing and dissolving

When we are in the kitchen cooking, we often mix things together. But not everything mixes in the same way. Some substances seem to disappear in water, while others don't mix at all.

Try stirring a spoonful of salt into a glass of cold water. Then try a spoonful of sugar, and then flour. Are the results of your test like those shown here?

Salt	Disappears. The water stays clear.
Sugar	Settles at the bottom. The water stays clear.
Flour	Mostly disappears. The water becomes cloudy.

The substances that seem to disappear have dissolved in the water. Things dissolve more easily in hot water, such as sugar in coffee.

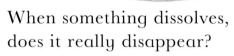

When something dissolves, does it really disappear? Dissolve some salt in water and taste it. The water is salty!

The salt is still there, and you can get it back. Leave a saucer of salty water in the sun. The water will slowly evaporate and leave the salt behind. Taste it and see!

💡 Lots of energy

We can't always see energy, but we can see its effects.

Energy makes things go. A sailboat uses wind energy to skim across the water. You use energy from the food you eat.

There are many forms of energy.

light

sound

heat

electricity

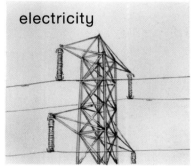

chemical energy—
        from
        food

chemical
energy—
from gas

What gives us energy?

We get nearly all our energy from the Sun.

For instance, grass uses the Sun's energy to grow. Cows eat grass, and this gives them energy to produce milk. We drink the milk, and this gives us energy to live and grow.

Millions of years ago, long before there were any humans, plants and animals were using the Sun's energy. When they died, their remains slowly turned into oil. We drill for oil and turn it into gas and diesel for cars. So a car runs on the Sun's energy.

Saving energy

Most of the energy we use comes from coal, oil, or gas. These fuels are called fossil fuels, and they have stored energy from the Sun for millions of years.

oil

gas

coal

We get fossil fuels from under the ground, but eventually the Earth's supply will run out. And there is another problem. When we burn fossil fuels in cars and power plants, they give off gases that pollute the air.

We must do everything we can to save energy, so that fuels last longer and there is less pollution. We can all help to do this.

We can turn off lights when they are not needed. A shower uses less hot water than a bath. We can stop wasting heat by closing windows and insulating houses. And we can recycle our garbage, not throw it away.

insulation

Everyday electricity

Electricity is very important in our everyday world. Think of all the things that stop working if there is a power cut.

There are two kinds of electricity. One is called static electricity. It is made by rubbing materials together. You can rub things yourself to see the effects of static. What happens if you comb your hair hard?

Your hair crackles with static and sticks up. Or rub a balloon on your jumper and watch it stick to the wall afterwards.

Electricity that travels along wires is called current electricity. **Warning!** *Electricity can kill you. Never play with switches, outlets, or anything that is plugged in.*

Circuits and switches

Electricity needs a pathway to flow around. We call this path a circuit. As long as the circuit is complete, electricity will flow.

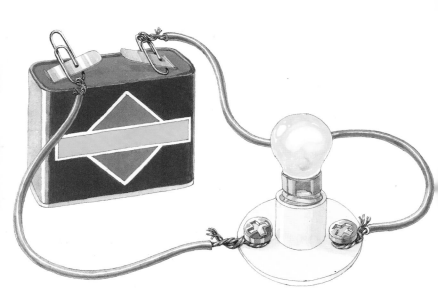

Electricity flows along a wire from one end, or terminal, of the battery. It passes through the bulb and lights it up. Then it travels back to the other battery terminal.

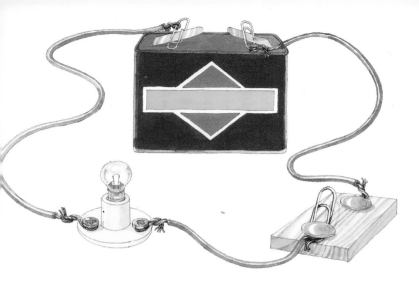

If there is a gap in the circuit, electricity
cannot flow. A switch works by connecting
the circuit to turn things on, and breaking
the circuit to turn things off.
In this circuit, a paper clip is the switch.
If it connects the circuit, the bulb lights up.
If it breaks the circuit, the bulb goes out.

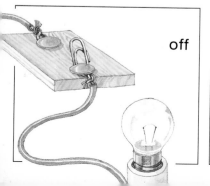

off

on

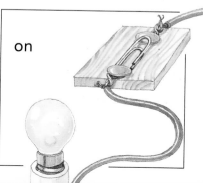

Gravity and weight

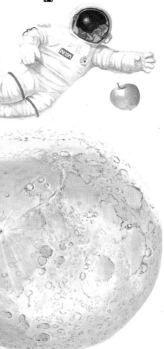

The Earth pulls everything toward its center, including us! This force is called gravity. It is the reason that things fall down and not up. You can throw a ball high in the air, but it will always fall back to the ground.

The Earth's gravity pulls on the Moon too, and keeps it circling around the Earth. But in Space there is so little gravity that things just float around, including astronauts.

The weight of any object depends on gravity. Scales measure the pull of the Earth's gravity on an object. We call this pull its weight.

4 oz.

The Moon's gravity is much less than the Earth's gravity. So a baby who weighs twelve pounds on Earth would only weigh two pounds on the Moon!

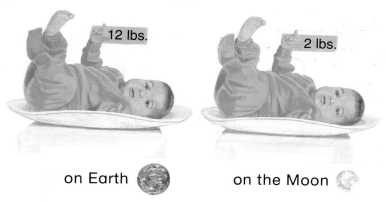

12 lbs.

2 lbs.

on Earth   on the Moon

Sticking and slipping

Have you ever slipped on a wet floor? If so, you slipped because there wasn't enough friction. Friction is a force that tries to stop things from slipping over each other. A bath mat increases friction and keeps you from slipping.

That is because rough surfaces produce more friction than smooth surfaces do.

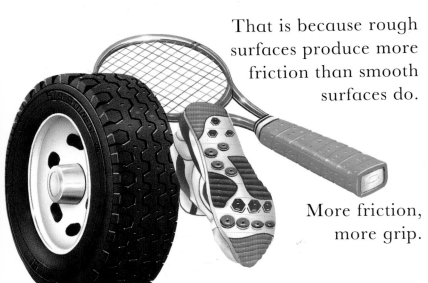

More friction, more grip.

Water is slippery. When you ride on a toboggan, the pressure melts a thin layer of snow underneath. This makes the toboggan slide more smoothly and quickly.

We put oil in a car's engine so that its parts run more smoothly. Friction causes heat—rub your hands together hard to feel this for yourself. So oil also keeps the engine from getting too hot.

Magnets

Magnets pull some materials toward them. A magnet will pull, or attract, a paper clip, for example. But some materials are not magnetic and will not be attracted.

To find out which materials are magnetic, test things with a magnet. Does your magnet attract anything that is not made of metal?

Every magnet has two ends called poles— a north and a south pole. Close together, the north pole of one magnet will attract the south pole of the other. But two of the same pole will push apart!

The Earth is like a giant magnet. It has a magnetic north pole and a magnetic south pole. The poles of your magnet are attracted to the Earth's magnetic poles.

The needle inside a compass is a magnet. It swings around to show where north is.

You can make a compass by magnetizing a needle. Stroke the needle in the same direction about 50 times with one end of your magnet. Tape the needle to a flat cork and float it in water. The ends of your needle will point north and south!

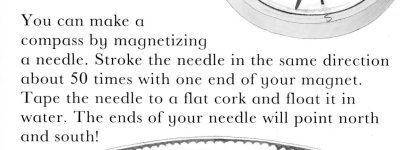

What is sound?

A sound is made by something vibrating—moving back and forth very quickly. As you speak, vibrations from your voice travel through air in sound waves.

To feel the vibrations, press a balloon to the front of a speaker. If you turn the sound up, can you feel more vibrations?

You can't see sound, but you can see its effects. Put some rice on a homemade drum, and bang on a tin lid. Sound makes the rice bounce!

There is no sound in Space, because there is no air for sound waves to travel in. Astronauts talk to each other by radio.

Sound travels well through liquids and solids. Male sea lions bark loudly under water to keep other males away.

 Color

Sunlight seems to be colorless or white. But it is really made up of several colors mixed together. You can see these colors in a rainbow, when sunlight passes through raindrops and gets split up. The seven colors in a rainbow are red, orange, yellow, green, blue, indigo, and violet.

Can you mix these colors back together, to get white?

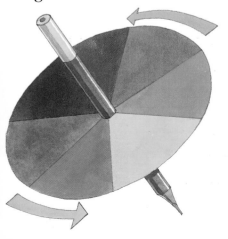

Cut a circle out of posterboard and divide it into seven sections. Color the sections with the colors of the rainbow. Put a pencil through the middle and spin the circle. What happens to the colors?

A prism splits light into different colors.
You can make your own
prism with a piece of cardboard
and a glass of water.

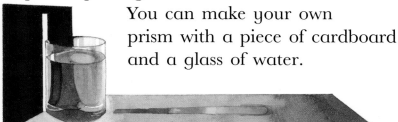

Cut a slit in the cardboard and place it up against
a window, with the glass of water in front of it.
You'll see the colors more clearly if you have
a sheet of white paper underneath.

Things are different colors because they
soak up some colors and let others bounce
off them. A banana lets yellow bounce
off it and soaks up other colors.
We see in full color, but
some animals only see in
shades of black and white.

265

Reflections

The Moon gives off no light of its own, but
sometimes we see it shining at night. This is
because light from the Sun bounces off the
Moon. Then we see the Moon, even though
we can't see the Sun! We might see this
"moonlight" reflected again on water.

When light hits any smooth, shiny surface, it bounces back and makes a reflection. When you look into a mirror, light bounces back at you and you see yourself.

Have you noticed that reflections are always reversed?

Mirrors are made of a sheet of glass in front of a thin piece of shiny metal.

A lot of other shiny surfaces reflect light.

Tricks of the light

If you put a straw in a glass of water, it seems to bend at the surface of the water. This effect is called refraction.

Refraction is caused by light traveling at different speeds through different materials. It moves faster through air than through water. When it changes speed, it changes direction slightly, too.

Put a coin in a glass of water and look at it from several angles. It seems to change shape and size, all because of refraction.

Refraction can make things look bigger, too. That's why a goldfish in a bowl seems to grow in size as it swims toward you!

The round goldfish bowl is made of curved glass, which can also bend light rays by refraction.

A magnifying glass is useful if we want to see things close up. The curved lens of glass increases the refraction so the coin looks bigger.

Amazing facts

Long ago, scientists called alchemists tried to change ordinary metals into precious gold. They never succeeded!

Geologists (scientists who study the Earth) think that there is enough oil under the ground to give us energy for about 40 years, enough gas for 55 years, and enough coal for 200 years.

How do birds find their way when they migrate across thousands of miles? Scientists think their brains contain magnetic iron that acts like a compass.

There is hardly any gravity in Space. Without Earth's gravity to weigh them down, astronauts grow a little taller in Space.

How Things are Made

A woolen sweater

Woolen clothes are made from the hair of animals such as sheep. The sheep's wool is called its fleece.

The shearer cuts the wool from the sheep with sharp clippers.

Shearing is like a haircut and does not hurt. The sheep soon grows a new fleece.

The wool is cleaned and spun into long threads called yarn. Then the wool is colored with dye.

People buy balls of yarn for knitting clothes.

This person is following a pattern for a sweater. It shows her how much yarn she needs and which kind of knitting needles and stitches to use.

 # Silk

silkworm

Silk is another material that comes from an animal. The silkworm is a caterpillar that spins a cocoon of silk around itself. It turns into a moth and hatches out from the cocoon.

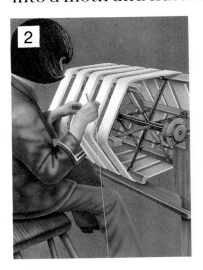

Farmers sell the cocoons to the silk factory.

At the factory, the cocoons are unraveled, and their silk is wound into thread on reeling frames. The thread is soaked in dye and woven into cloth on a loom.

silkworm spinning   cocoon   adult moth

Silk is a beautiful material. It is used all over the world to make clothes for special occasions.

Japanese kimono, for festivals

Indian sari, for dancing

Made of plastic

Thousands of things are made of plastic,
perhaps even some of your clothes.

rig

Plastic is made from oil.
Oil is found underground.
Giant rigs drill deep holes in
the ground. The oil flows up
the pipes inside the hole. It is
called crude oil. It goes by
pipeline or by tanker to the
oil refinery.

crude oil refinery

The refinery heats the crude oil
to separate the chemicals in it.
These chemicals make useful
things such as gasoline and
plastics.

There are many kinds of plastic
– hard plastics and soft,
bendable plastics. A soft plastic
called PVC is made from one of
the chemicals in crude oil and
from salt.

salt

277

At the glassworks

The main ingredients in glass are a type of sand called silica, bits of scrap glass called cullet, soda ash, and limestone. They are mixed together and heated in a furnace until they melt and turn into molten glass.

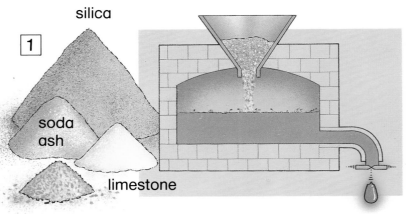

silica

1

soda ash

limestone

cullet

Rollers press the hot liquid glass into a flat sheet. The glass hardens as it cools. It is used to make windowpanes.

2

Glass jars and bottles are made in a different way.

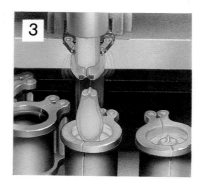

As the molten glass flows from the furnace, it is cut into blobs called gobs. Each gob drops into a mold.

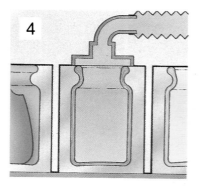

A blast of air presses the glass against the sides of this mold, in the shape of a jar.

The mold opens. Tongs pick up the jar and put it into a big oven called a lehr. The lehr heats the glass again, to make it stronger.

The glass blower

Some glass is made by hand. This is a skilled job.

The gatherer picks up a gob of molten glass on a long tube.

The blower blows down the tube to fill the gob with air and make it swell up like a balloon.

The blower keeps turning the tube so the glass doesn't drip off. He squeezes the end of the gob with tongs, to make a long stem. The foot setter adds another gob to the stem and flattens it into a base called a foot.

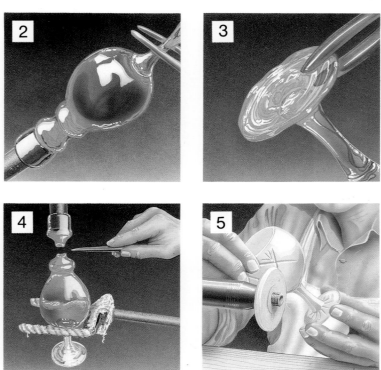

The cutter takes the glass and smooths it with a grinder. He cuts the glass with a sharp, whirring wheel to make a pattern.

Breakfast cereal

Cornflakes are made from sweet corn. When the corn has ripened in the sun, farmers harvest their crop.

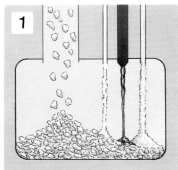

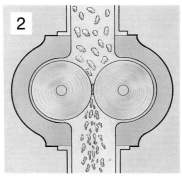

Grains of corn are stripped from the plants and taken to a cereal factory. At the factory, sugar, salt, and malt flavoring are added to the corn to give it extra taste. Next, the mixture is cooked. Then heavy rollers press the corn into flakes.

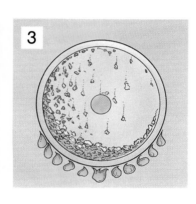

The flakes are toasted in giant ovens to make them crispy.

Filling machines weigh the cornflakes into bags. The bags are sealed to keep the cornflakes fresh.

Conveyor belts take the bags to be packed in boxes. The boxes are put in big cardboard cartons, to protect them on their way to the stores.

▰ Fizzy drinks

Oranges and other fruit give many fizzy drinks a delicious taste. Pickers pull the fruit from the trees.

Juice is squeezed from the fruit and packed in drums.

Ships take the juice to other countries.

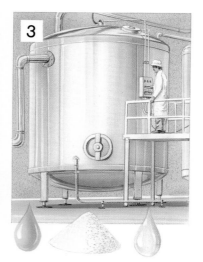

At the factory, sugar, water, and other ingredients are added to the juice. In a high-pressure tank, a gas called carbon dioxide is forced into the mixture, to give it sparkling bubbles.

A can-filling machine squirts the drink into 8,000 cans each minute. A machine called a seamer puts the lids on.

A soda can

Cans are made of metal, often a metal called steel. Steel comes from iron ore under the ground. Miners dig up the ore.

At the steel mill, huge furnaces heat the iron ore to turn it into liquid iron and then liquid steel. As the liquid cools and hardens, rolling mills flatten it into sheets of steel. Factories buy the steel to make cans.

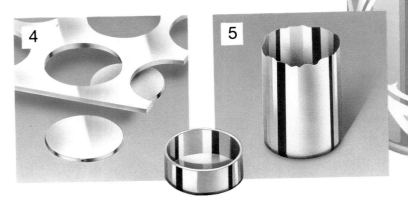

At the factory, a press pushes small disks out of the steel sheet. An ironing machine stretches each disk into a can shape. Printing rollers add color. Another machine shapes the top of the can where the lid will fit.

Toothpaste

Toothpaste is made from this mixture:

- hydrated silica, to polish your teeth,

- sorbitol, made from plants, for binding the mixture into a paste,

- a foaming agent, to make the toothpaste frothy,

- mint, or other flavors, for a fresh taste and smell,

- water, to turn the mixture into a soft paste,

FLUORIDE

- and fluoride, to help prevent tooth decay.

The ingredients are mixed in a vat and poured into tubes. A red light shows when each tube is full. Then the tubes are closed and packed in cartons.

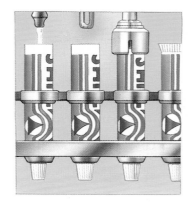

In striped toothpaste, colored paste is put in first. Then white paste fills the rest of the tube.

When you squeeze the tube, the white paste comes out through a nozzle in the center, and the colored paste comes through holes around the edge.

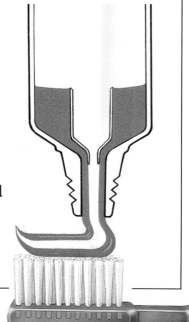

Amazing facts

One silkworm can make almost 5,000 feet of silk thread in its cocoon.

Wool comes not just from sheep, but from goats, camels, yaks, llamas, and rabbits too.

Peanuts are not just good to eat. They can also be used to make soap and ink.

The first paper was made from reed plants in Ancient Egypt over 5,000 years ago. The word paper comes from the name of the reeds, papyrus.

On the Move

✳ A bicycle

On a bicycle you use your feet to move the pedals. Follow the numbers to find out what happens next.

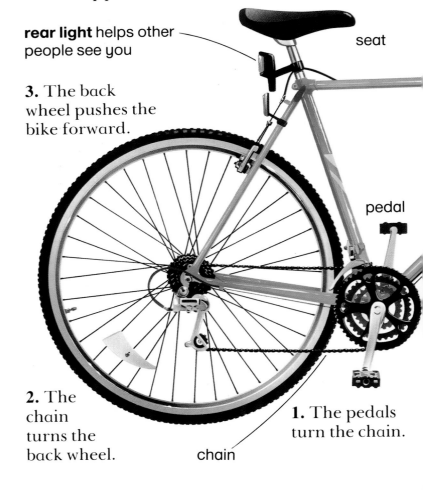

rear light helps other people see you

seat

3. The back wheel pushes the bike forward.

pedal

2. The chain turns the back wheel.

1. The pedals turn the chain.

chain

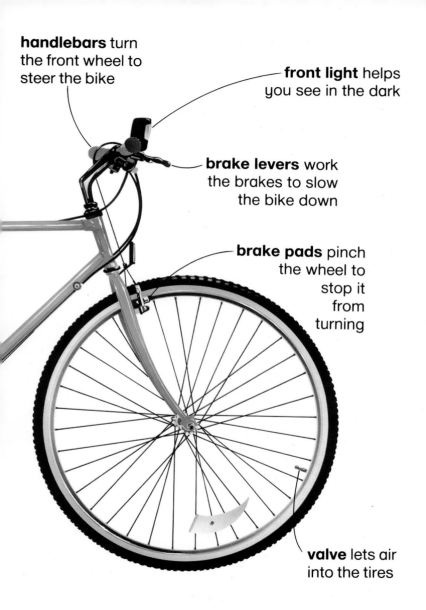

handlebars turn the front wheel to steer the bike

front light helps you see in the dark

brake levers work the brakes to slow the bike down

brake pads pinch the wheel to stop it from turning

valve lets air into the tires

 A car

A car has hundreds of parts. It has a strong metal frame, called a chassis, and a body made of thin metal panels. Follow the numbers to see how it works.

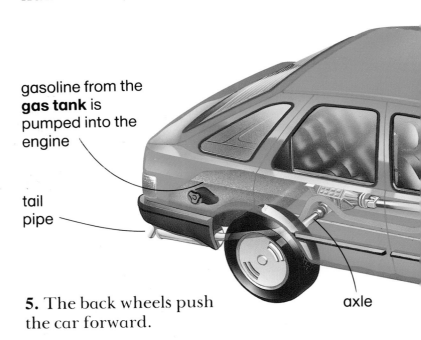

gasoline from the **gas tank** is pumped into the engine

tail pipe

axle

5. The back wheels push the car forward.

In some cars the engine turns the front wheels. This is called front-wheel drive.

4. The drive shaft turns the axle, and this turns the back wheels.

1. Turning the key starts the engine.

2. Gasoline in the engine is mixed with air. Electric sparks make the mixture explode over and over again, pushing pistons up and down.

windshield

battery

radiator helps cool the engine

drive shaft

engine

3. The pistons turn the drive shaft.

front disc brakes

A tractor-trailer

trailer carries the load

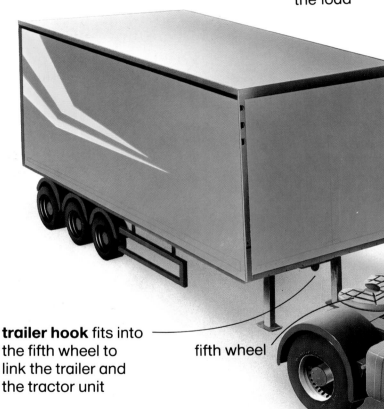

trailer hook fits into the fifth wheel to link the trailer and the tractor unit

fifth wheel

diesel fuel for the engine is carried in the **fuel tank**

A tractor-trailor is made up of two parts: a trailer and a tractor. The trailer is like a big container. It has no engine and is pulled along by the tractor. Because a tractor-trailer is made up of two parts, it can go around tight corners.

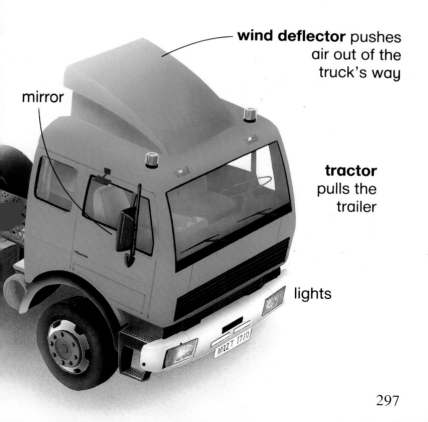

wind deflector pushes air out of the truck's way

mirror

tractor pulls the trailer

lights

✵ A steam train

A steam train burns wood or coal to heat water and make steam. The steam then pushes pistons that turn the wheels.

This steam train traveled across North America over 100 years ago. The cowcatcher in front cleared the track.

✸ Trains around the world

Steam trains are still used on some railroads. This one is in India.

A modern diesel-electric train burns oil to make electricity. The electricity drives the train's motors.

A cog railway is designed to climb steep hills. It has an extra wheel with teeth that fit into notches on a third rail. This stops the train from slipping down the hill.

third rail

✳ All kinds of ships

Ships come in different shapes and sizes.

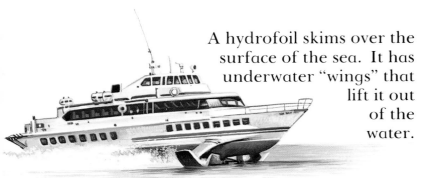

A hydrofoil skims over the surface of the sea. It has underwater "wings" that lift it out of the water.

Hovercraft float on a cushion of air. Hidden fans blow air downward and lift the hovercraft off the water.

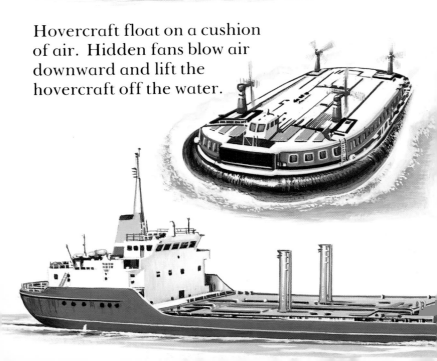

Paddle steamers travel up
and down rivers.
They are
driven by a
big wheel at
the stern.

Lifeboats rescue people at
sea. They are small, but
they are almost
unsinkable.

Fishing trawlers have a
winding engine at the
stern to haul in
their heavy nets.

Supertankers carry oil
in huge tanks. They
are the biggest ships
in the world.

✵ A submarine

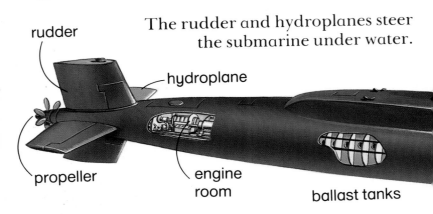

The rudder and hydroplanes steer the submarine under water.

rudder

hydroplane

propeller

engine room

ballast tanks

Submarines are ships that go under water. They can stay under water for weeks without coming to the surface. The commander controls the submarine from the control room. By raising the periscope, he can look around above the water.

ballast tanks are flooded with water

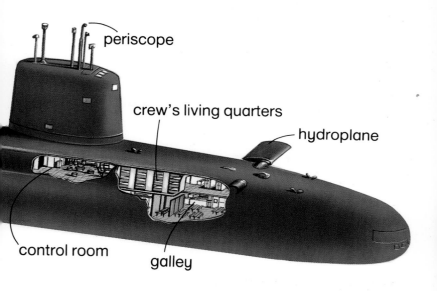

periscope

crew's living quarters

hydroplane

control room

galley

To dive, the submarine's ballast tanks are flooded with seawater. The submarine sinks. To come back up to the surface, air is blown into the ballast tanks, pushing out the water.

ballast tanks full of water

air pushes water out of tanks

✳ A jumbo jet

This Boeing 747 is the world's biggest
passenger plane. It has room for about 400
passengers. Its four turbofan engines push
it through the air at over 550 miles an
hour. It has a wide body, called the
fuselage, thin strong
wings, and a big tailfin.

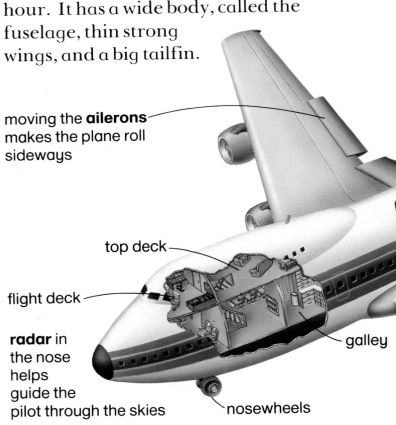

moving the **ailerons**
makes the plane roll
sideways

top deck

flight deck

radar in
the nose
helps
guide the
pilot through the skies

galley

nosewheels

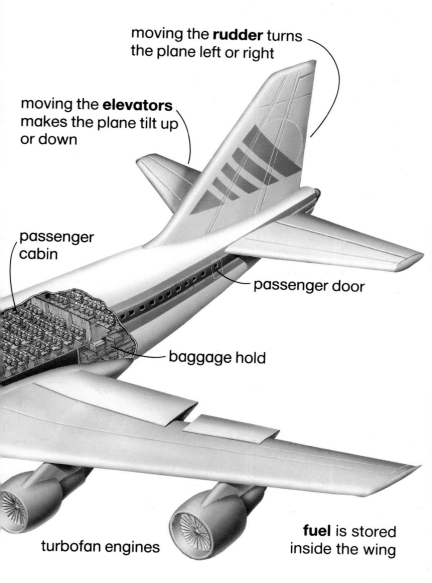

moving the **rudder** turns the plane left or right

moving the **elevators** makes the plane tilt up or down

passenger cabin

passenger door

baggage hold

turbofan engines

fuel is stored inside the wing

✺ How a plane flies

As the engines drive the plane along the runway, air flows around the wings. The faster the plane goes, the faster the air flows.

The forward push that comes from the engines is called thrust.

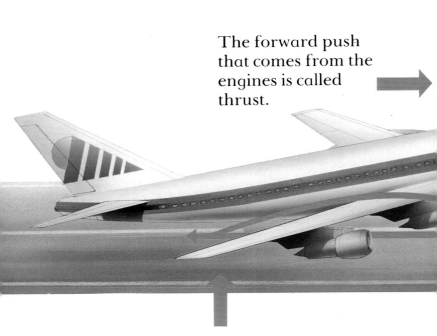

Air flowing over and under the curved wing creates lift.

The upward push is called lift.

The wings of a plane have a curved shape. When air flows over and under the wings, it creates an upward push beneath the plane. As the plane picks up speed, the upward push gets stronger. When it is strong enough, it lifts the plane off the ground.

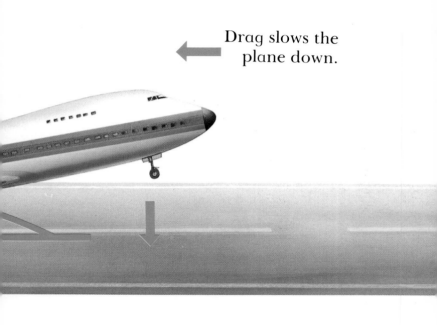

Drag slows the plane down.

The weight of the plane pulls it downward.

✳ Helicopters

A helicopter has spinning rotor blades instead of wings. It can fly upward or downward or sideways and can even hover in midair.

To move the helicopter in all these different directions, the pilot changes the angle of the rotor blades using a joy stick and foot pedals.

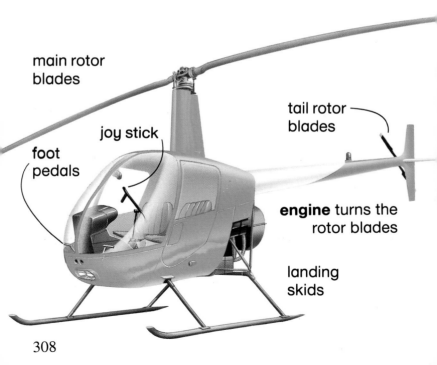

main rotor blades

tail rotor blades

joy stick

foot pedals

engine turns the rotor blades

landing skids

Helicopters are often used to rescue people at sea. The pilot keeps the helicopter steady while one of the crew members is lowered on a line to help the person in the water. Then both are winched up to safety.

✸ The space shuttle

The living area and the flight deck are in
the nose of the shuttle. In the middle is the
payload bay. Once the shuttle is out in
space, the doors of the payload bay can
open. On this mission the shuttle is carrying
a telescope and a spacelab.

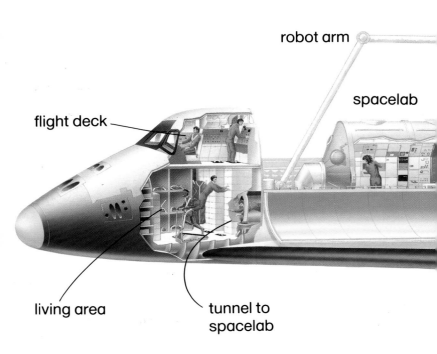

robot arm

spacelab

flight deck

living area

tunnel to
spacelab

The astronauts carry out scientific experiments in the lab. One of the astronauts is working out in the payload bay. He is attached to a robot arm so he doesn't float away.

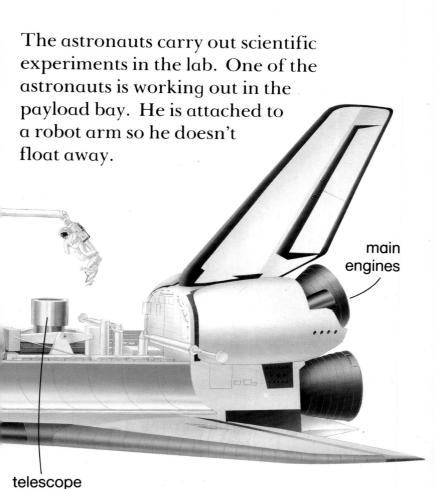

main engines

telescope

small **thruster rockets** move the shuttle while it is in space

Amazing facts

✳ The wheel was the first important invention in transportation. People first made wheels over 5,000 years ago by fastening pieces of wood together.

✳ There are more than 500 million cars in the world. About one third of them are driven in North America.

✳ In 1933, Wiley Post became the first person to fly solo around the world. His journey was 15,596 miles long and took 7 days, 18 hours, and 49 minutes.

✳ The world's first human space traveler was Yuri Gagarin of the U.S.S.R. He traveled once around the earth in 1961. The first people to land on the Moon were American astronauts Neil Armstrong and Edwin Aldrin. They landed in the *Apollo 11* spacecraft on July 21, 1969.

INDEX

Acknowledgments

Authors
Michael Benton, Michael Chinery, Fabienne Fustec, Sian Hardy, Dominique Joly, Keith Lye, Christopher Maynard, Nina Morgan, Steve Parker, Barbara Reseigh, Dominique Rist, Jean-Pierre Verdet, Florence Wessels, Pierre-Olivier Wessels

Consultants
Dr. Jean-Baptiste Carlander, Michael Chinery, Brenda Cook, Daphne Ingram, Jean-Noël Labat, Denise Larpin, James Muirden, Nigel Nelson, Sally Purkis, Brian Williams

Illustrators
Marion Appleton, Craig Austin, John Barber, Denise Bazin, Pierre Bon, Maggie Brand, Derek Brazell, Brighton Illustration Agency, Jim Channell, Bob Corley, Peter Dennis, Bernard Duhem, Jean-Philippe Duponq, Luc Favreau, Diane Fawcett, Catherine Fichaux, Andrew French, Louis R. Galante, Tony Gibbons, Peter Goodfellow, Graffito, Terry Hadler, Rebecca Hardy, Nick Hawken, Tim Hayward, Pierre Hezard, Kay Hodges, Ian Jackson, David Kearney, Tony Kenyon, Marc Lagarde, Terence Lambert, Gilbert Macé, Kevin Maddison, Alan Male, Shirley Mallinson, David McAllister, Florence McKenzie, Barry Mitchell, Oxford Illustrators, Jean-Marc Pau, François Pichon, Stephen Player, Larry Rostant, Danièle Schulthess, Stephen Seymour, Etienne Souppart, John Spires, Valérie Stetten, Roger Stewart (Kevin Jones Associates), Eva Styner, Swanston Graphics, Treve Tamblin, Lawrie Taylor, Jean Torton, Michèle Trumel, Vincent Wakerley, Graham White, Ann Winterbotham, David Wright, Paul Young